# THE MARINE CORPS
# IN VIETNAM

TEXT BY
CHARLES D. MELSON

COLOUR PLATES BY
RAMIRO BUJEIRO

OSPREY
HISTORY

First published in Great Britain in 1998 by Osprey Publishing, Elms Court, Chapel Way, Botley, Oxford OX2 9LP, United Kingdom
Email: info@ospreypublishing.com

Also published as Warrior 23 *US Marine in Vietnam*

ISBN 1 84176 105 2

Military Editor: Iain MacGregor
Design: Alan Hamp @ Design for Books

Filmset in Singapore by Pica Ltd.
Printed in China through World Print Ltd.

FOR A CATALOGUE OF ALL BOOKS PUBLISHED BY OSPREY MILITARY, AUTOMOTIVE AND AVIATION PLEASE WRITE TO:

The Marketing Manager, Osprey Direct UK, PO Box 140, Wellingborough, Northants, NN8 4ZA, United Kingdom
Email: info@ospreydirect.co.uk

The Marketing Manager, Osprey Direct USA, PO Box 130, Sterling Heights, MI 48311-0130, United States of America
Email: info@ospreydirectusa.com

FRONT COVER: Marine infantry Rifleman (DOD)

BACK COVER: US Marine Corps 1st Tank Bn. vehicle with the 5th Marines south-west of Da Nang (USMC)

## Author's Dedication

For Janet, David and Katherine.

For the Walking Dead, brothers by service not birth, and the 14,809 Marines who died in Southeast Asia. – *Semper Fidelis!*

These events are historical, but squad-level personae and incidents are reconstructions and any resemblance to the living or the dead is coincidental. Quotations are from sources cited and the Marine Corps Gazette. Permission to reproduce material was granted by Alfred A. Knopf, Doubleday, and Random House. Photographs and graphics are from the Department of Defense (DOD), the US Naval Institute (USNI) and the Marine Corps Historical Collection (MCHC). Thanks to Diane Blazejak for the cover photograph, and to Col. E.R. (Sonny) Laine Jr. USMC (Ret), Charles R. Smith, Gordan Rottman and Kevin Lyles for their help.

*Our destinies are sometimes focused on the small point of a bayonet.*
 – John F. Kennedy

# THE MARINE CORPS IN VIETNAM

## INTRODUCTION

### The Corps and the War

**The Drill Instructor was the non-commissioned officer charged with the conversion of civilians into enlisted Marines at the recruit depots, the boot camps in South Carolina on the East Coast and California on the West Coast. The old-fashioned campaign hat was symbolic of the position. (USNI)**

Portrayed are US Marine riflemen as they "locate, close with, and destroy the enemy by fire and maneuver, or repel the enemy's assaults by fire and close combat". In this volume we follow fictional fire-team members through enlistment, training, battle and return during the war's climax. This is a representative account, if not a specific one, to answer the veteran's touchstone questions: "Who were you with?" and "When were you there?" It is about men in combat against the enemies of their country and tells in part the story of the 1st Company, 1st Battalion, 9th Regiment of Marines during a mobile operation in the western highlands on the border of Vietnam and Laos in early 1969.

Since 10 November 1775 the American Marines have viewed themselves as light infantry, complete with green uniforms, black accoutrements and, for a time, a hunting-horn emblem (a French horn rather than a German bugle). In various forms the Marines served in most of the declared and undeclared US conflicts "from the halls of Montezuma to the shores of Tripoli". Two brigades served in Europe in World War One and six divisions, along with aviation and supporting troops, battled in the Pacific during World War Two. A national defence act in 1947 established the modern Marine Corps: three amphibious divisions, three aircraft wings and a reserve. This settled the Corps' position within the defence structure at a fixed minimum size. Major bases were at Quantico, Virginia; Camp Lejeune, North Carolina; Camp Pendleton, California; and throughout the Pacific region. Headquarters were in Arlington, Virginia, outside Washington D.C.

Starting in 1950, Marines served in Korea, Indo-China, Lebanon, Cuba, Laos, Haiti, and the Dominican Republic. The Cold War turned into an era of numerous 'hot' conflicts that stopped short of general or even limited war. After the withdrawal of France from Indo-China and the partition of Vietnam into north and south pending elections, the Americans moved to help the Republic of South Vietnam against the People's Republic of Vietnam in the north. The civil war that ensued had international implications that involved several world powers and their clients.

By 1960, the date on the Vietnam Campaign Medal, a state of armed conflict existed between the two Vietnams and their allies. Marine advisors were present in South Vietnam and the first tactical units sent were Marine helicopter squadrons in 1962. The landing of the 9th Marine Expeditionary Brigade at Da Nang in March 1965 ensured large-scale Marine Corps involvement.

When the commitment in Southeast Asia began, the US Marines were well trained, organised and equipped for orthodox operations. They were confronted in South Vietnam by what Marine Gen. Lewis W. Walt characterised as a "strange war, strange strategy". The conflict displayed a full spectrum of violence, from individual terrorism and guerrilla fighting to conventional land combat with extensive sea and air components. All of this was within the context of diplomatic and domestic politics of the various parties in Vietnam at the time.

The US Marines mainly operated in I Corps, the northernmost of the South Vietnamese regions bordering Laos, North Vietnam and the South China Sea. From the west, valleys and ridges served as infiltration routes for Communists attacking coastal population zones, and these same hinterlands served as enemy rear and staging areas.

In 1965 the Marines organised the coastal enclaves and took an expanding 'oil spot' approach to operations from Da Nang and Chu Lai. By 1967 North Vietnamese build-ups along the demilitarised zone (DMZ) were met by Marines in a defensive posture that carried through until 1968, with decisive confrontations at Khe Sanh, Dong Ha and Hue City. By mid-1968 allied forces held, and Marines used a mobile approach to 'search and destroy' Communist forces. This continued into 1969. The Marines began to leave that year as the South Vietnamese assumed a larger role in the fighting and most US units were gone by July 1971. Fighting continued until the eventual defeat of the South Vietnamese by the North and the subsequent change of regional order in 1975. The conflict, the longest in the history of the Corps, exacted a high cost, with more than 14,800 Marines killed and 88,000 wounded. It is against a background of two decades of war that this account should be viewed.

With drill, weapons training, and uniform inspections came a requirement for cleanliness and order that saw frequent 'field days' by recruits to keep barracks free from dirt and dust. Worn is the scarlet and gold athletic uniform referred to as the 'Mickey Mouse' outfit. (DOD)

# CHRONOLOGY

### 1961
Direct US military aid to South Vietnam begins.

### 1964
US warships attacked in the Gulf of Tonkin. President Lyndon Johnson calls for action.

### 1965
US bases attacked in South Vietnam. Tactical bombing of North Vietnam begins, and US Marines land, along with army units.

### 1966
Strategic bombing of North Vietnam begins and US ground forces continue to build up, including Marines at Da Nang and Chu Lai.

## 1967

Heavy fighting by army near Saigon and Marines move to defend the demilitarised zone.

## 1968

*January–April* Defence of Khe Sanh by Marines. Tet offensive launched throughout South Vietnam, with fighting in Saigon and Hue.

*March–May* Bombing restricted by Americans, with renewed attacks and negotiation offers by the Communists.

*November* Bombing halt in North Vietnam. Richard Nixon elected president.

## 1969

*January* Truce negotiations begin in Paris. US forces in Vietnam at a peak of 542,400.

*July* Planned withdrawal of US troops begins.

*November* Massive anti-war demonstrations in America.

**Physical fitness formed a part of the programme designed to rapidly build up recruits through exercise and nutrition. The instructor on the right looks for an aggressive attitude. The recruits wear combat boots, utility trousers, and grey sweat shirts. (USNI)**

## 1970

*March* US and South Vietnamese invade Cambodia.

*May* Violent anti-war demonstrations in America.

*June–July* Withdrawals from Cambodia.

*December* Congress repeals Tonkin Gulf resolutions.

## 1971

*February–March* South Vietnamese invade Laos. US force reductions continue.

*July* Last Marine combat units depart.

## 1972

*March* North Vietnamese invade South Vietnam, bombing of North Vietnam resumes and Americans support returns.

*May* North Vietnam ports mined and bombing increased.

*August* Last US combat forces depart South Vietnam, leaving 43,000 support personnel.

## 1973

*January* Peace agreement signed between US and North Vietnam.

*March* Remaining US forces depart South Vietnam.

# ENLISTMENT

## The Human Factor

An estimated 500,000 Marines served in Vietnam from 1962 through to 1975. In 1968 Marines numbered 85,881, from more than 501,000 Americans under the Military Advisory Command Vietnam. By then, those joining the armed forces or conscripted by selective service knew the prospect of combat was not a matter of if, but when. The Commandant of the Marine Corps at the time, Gen. Leonard F. Chapman, stated that there were three kinds of Marines: "those in Vietnam, those who had just come back from Vietnam, and those who were getting ready to go to Vietnam".

The average Marine was an 18- or 19-year-old male with a high school education, from an urban working class or rural small town background, and of an economic and racial mix that was more varied than American society as a whole. Motivation for enlistment was patriotism, self-advancement, personal reasons and the looming prospect of being drafted (about 20,000 Marines were conscripted during the war).

Members of the high school Class of 1968 not deferred from the draft often ended up with local recruiters who used fabled sales techniques, guaranteeing that "The Marine Corps Builds Men". This might be bolstered by family histories of military service and Hollywood images from *The Sands of Iwo Jima* or *Victory at Sea* for background. However, this was tempered by graphic television images and combat veterans returning – wounded and dead – from the conflict.

One new recruit was Joe Benotz, whose failure to manage car payments, a girlfriend and college classes found him walking into the Marine Corps store front in Watertown, New York, and signing up to be one of America's finest. The Marines offered a two-year enlistment with the same obligations as the draft, and Benotz felt that "if you were going to have to fight, then you might as well be trained by the best". This entailed a quick four months of preparation, usually followed by a Vietnam tour. Whatever the recruit's reasons for joining up, the Marine Corps Recruit Depot (MCRD) quickly made logic irrelevant with the shock of the 'boot camp' and the overriding rigours of day-to-day service.

Pte.s Benotz, Valdez, and Murphy learned the spirit of the bayonet was to 'Kill, Kill, Kill' as recruits demonstrate with M14 rifles and bayonets. Pugnacity was demanded during bayonet training both as a drill and during 'pugil stick' bouts with padded 'rifles' and protective equipment. (USNI)

RIGHT **After graduation from boot camp, Marines assigned to the infantry went on to training for the various specialities from rifleman to crew-served weapons. In this case an instructor lectures on the use of the 60mm mortar to students wearing helmets with camouflage covers. They wear M62 utility uniforms. (DOD)**

# TRAINING

Limited field training was conducted as part of the recruit process, primarily in the form of conditioning hikes with packs and rifles. This drill instructor carries the M41 pack with blanket roll to set the example for his heavily laden charges at left. (USNI)

## Recruit Depot and Infantry Training Regiment

San Diego, California, and Parris Island, South Carolina, were the processing centres for civilians seeking entry into the Corps' ranks. Recruit depots were to "receive, degrade, sanitise, immunise, cloth, equip, train, pain, scold, mould, sand and polish" according to former Commandant Gen. David M. Shoup. Recruits were trained by methods that bear little comparison with any other profession, avocation, or sport: they had to learn to leave a place of comparative safety, on order, and to go towards an armed enemy "whose purpose in life is to kill you". This was imparted with the fundamentals of drill, physical training and marksmanship. The 10 weeks allocated to initial training were divided rigidly into Receiving, Forming, and Phases I, II and III.

Regardless of the initial terms of entry or final assignment, all enlisted Marines went through this training process (and officers endured their own version of it at Quantico, Virginia). Training was administered by enlisted drill instructors, whose creed stated: "I will train them to the best of my ability. I will develop them into smartly disciplined, physically fit, basically trained Marines, thoroughly indoctrinated in love of corps and country." This was sublimated to: "Be damned sure no man's ghost returns to ask 'If your training programme had only done its job'."

Journalist William Mares, a reservist, wrote that by late 1968 the Marine Corps had had to adjust to replace the dead, wounded and discharged of the ranks. It had been forced "to reduce the length of training, increase the input of recruits and lower the mental and physical standards for enlistment". He concluded that these changes "put increased pressure on the teacher-priest-guard-father-mother hen most responsible for training the recruits – the DIs". This pressure was passed on to the 'Boots', who struggled to shed their civilian background faced with their new realities. "No one forced you to join. If you don't like it, then tough shit."

Pat Murphy, from Philadelphia, got the first view of his home for the next weeks through the greasy window of a bus in the middle of the night. What impressions he had were soon disrupted by a disembodied shout that emptied the bus with: "My name is Staff Sergeant Brown and I am a member of the finest fighting outfit in the world! You scum-bags have ten seconds to get off this bus, NOW!" Murphy and 38 others fought their way out the door and on to yellow footprints painted on the pavement. The shouting and prodding by khaki-clad instructors in 'Smokey-the-Bear' hats became familiar in the weeks to follow.

Receiving and forming was designed to process the incoming recruits rapidly into 75-man training platoons, under the supervision of a senior drill instructor and two assistant drill instructors as part of a four platoon 'series'. All were crammed into open 'squad bays' in old brick barracks or even older prefabricated huts. The recruits' personal space centred on a bed or 'rack', a foot locker and a wall locker.

A 'PX' (post exchange) issue included the essentials of bucket, brushes, towel, soap, razor, toothbrush, toothpaste, Brasso metal polish, Kiwi shoe polish, physical training clothing, consumable sundries and a *Guidebook for Marines* to cover any information the instructors might miss. Recruits also received clothing and equipment to be used and looked after. This included some 37 different pieces of uniform and clothing for dress, service and utility uniforms.

Individual combat equipment was known by Vietnam-era Marines as '782' gear. Fielded as Marine Corps M1941 individual combat equipment, the sturdy construction of canvas, webbing and brass fittings was almost indestructible. The marching, field marching, transport and field transport packs were memorised and assembled at boot camp, if nowhere else.

To make recruits more

**Pre-deployment training used jungle lane firing exercises, village search and clearing drills, and orientation to the weapons that would be encountered in Vietnam from captured stocks. These Marines handle the Communist-bloc hardware they might find in combat. (DOD)**

responsive to schedules, methods, and expectations it was necessary to disorient them. This was done by stripping them of clothing, possessions, hair and any false dignity they might have. Drill, speech, bodily functions and even personal hygiene was accomplished 'by the numbers' in an instructor-approved fashion. No area of human existence was too personal to be regulated. Compliance with the Marine Corps way was the only way: "a place for everything and everything in its place". Infractions were punished with warnings, physical exercise and group ridicule. If physical abuse was not condoned, it certainly existed, and recruits either functioned or failed under pressure.

Marines had to learn three things: a proper respect for lawful authority (how to obey orders); how to take care of themselves (maintenance of clothing, equipment and health); and how to live with fellow Marines (teamwork). The underlying theory was that the sooner these fundamentals were learned the better, for the longer they took to grasp, the more traumatic an experience it would be. The three weeks

Squad tents used as living quarters in a base camp in Vietnam, often with plywood flooring and wooden hardback frames. A Marine examines animal traps used as booby-traps by the Communists. He wears theatre-issued jungle utilities with M62 cover. (USNI)

of Phase I included drill, callisthenics, memorising orders, trying to wear the uniform and equipment, and cleaning and carrying an eight-and-a-half-pound M14 service rifle. Days began and ended with physical training by the numbers of the 'daily seven'. Marine historian and depot alumni Dr. V. Keith Fleming recalled: "Drill instructors ceaselessly stalk about the platoon, their anger ready to boil over as they scream and shout at the young privates."

The recruits, many of whom were far from their familiar neighbourhood for the first time, learned about their instructors and each other, and learned to depend upon others from diverse backgrounds. The goal was to understand the importance of collective discipline. They also learned hygiene, weapons, customs and courtesies, first aid and packs, through lectures, demonstrations and practical application.

Most of the training was reinforced on an informal level by the ever-present drill instructors, and competition with other platoons measured individual and collective performance. Proper 'motivation' was considered as important as actual knowledge or proficiency.

The three weeks of Phase II were devoted to using the rifle on a known distance range. This meant an intensive focus on a skill that distinguished Marines: the use of small arms in battle. With war in progress, recruits dedicated marksmanship training "to the VC, to give them a better chance to die" for their country (Mares). Together with their whole platoon, Murphy and Benotz recited MajGen W. H. Rupertus' creed, *My Rifle*: "This is my rifle. There are many like it, but this one is mine. My rifle is my best friend. It is my life. I must master it as I must master my life. My rifle, without me is useless. Without my rifle, I am useless!"

The tasks of nomenclature, marksmanship theory, snapping in drills and the qualification course were designed to enable Marines to hit the target at 200, 300 and 500 yards, and so turn them into marksmen, sharpshooters and expert riflemen. Success for 'dingers' was offset by the failure of others, the 'unqs', for not qualifying. Familiarisation with the pistol was taught in passing. Phase II ended with a week of 'mess and maintenance' duties that had the recruits work in the dining hall to feed other recruits – including women Marines sometimes.

Phase III primed the recruits for graduation and assignment – drill, examinations and swimming instruction (Marines were a seagoing service). Physical training focused on the readiness test, conditioning

**The field mess; Marines go through the scullery to wash and disinfect utensils in garbage cans of water heated by immersion burners. Sanitation was a concern, particularly in base areas that depended upon primitive measures to prevent disease or vermin from spreading. Rain suits were worn in the wet weather. (USNI)**

runs and hikes, and hand-to-hand combat. There would be an overnight in the field, a military field meet, a drill competition and maybe a platoon party to mark the end of training. Daily inspection ensured that the early lessons were not forgotten and that the proper esprit was being exhibited. The recruits who had not made it that far disappeared to motivation platoons, special training, series recycle or medical discharges.

In the series Mares followed, of 300 that started, about 240 graduated. Those that did not were enough in number to make those that remained feel like survivors entitled to be called Marines. Murphy and Benotz's drill instructor's parting words were: "Work as hard as you can. Don't suck ass. Be yourself. You are an ambassador of the United States and the Marine Corps. Good luck."

A short graduation parade and recognition of platoon and series 'Honor Men' marked the completion of this right-of-passage, with a pass-in-review to the sounds of John Philip Sousa's *Semper Fidelis*. Parents, girlfriends and others attended, and the new Marines were given a few hours off before they had to return to the barracks for the assignment of 'military occupational specialties' (MOSs) and further training at other locations. High school graduates went to aviation or communications schools; the less gifted went to service support assignments ("Why die? Go supply!"), and those in-between went to the combat arms. For half of the recruit platoon this meant the Infantry Training Regiments (ITRs) at Camp Pendleton or Lejeune. While tradition demanded that "every Marine is a rifleman", in practice only those assigned Occupational Field 03 were 'school trained' for this. The goal of the ITR was to produce riflemen, machine-gunners, mortar men, assault men and anti-tank assault men for Fleet Marine Force Pacific or Atlantic in just four weeks. There followed a year of combat for most, although a select few were picked for barracks, ship and embassy duties.

Infantry training was less intense and without the full-time presence of drill instructors; the infantry students were able to flex their new-found freedom and their pay cheques. Pay-day was bi-monthly, in cash, although a private's $1,383.40 annual pay did not go very far. Deductions were made for taxes, insurance, charities and lost equipment. Extra allowances were given for meals, dependants and uniforms, and they had to put aside enough to pay for haircuts, starch and boot polish.

Though it was still before dawn, the Quonset hut was sweltering as Juan Valdez woke to the sounds of his bunkmate barfing in the lower rack. The last bus from town was not the 'vomit comet' for nothing, he thought. Southern California was his home, and it did not hold the same fascination for him that it did for the others in his training platoon. Patrick Murphy had come back to the San Onofre area with a hangover and a bloody tattoo that proclaimed 'Death Before Dishonor' on his right arm. This might be worth a run to the top of the hill known as 'Old Smokey' and back if an instructor noticed it.

Civic action maintained good relations with the Vietnamese civilians in the populated base areas. A medical corpsman takes advantage of purified water supplies to allow local children to bath as a treatment of endemic skin conditions. (DOD)

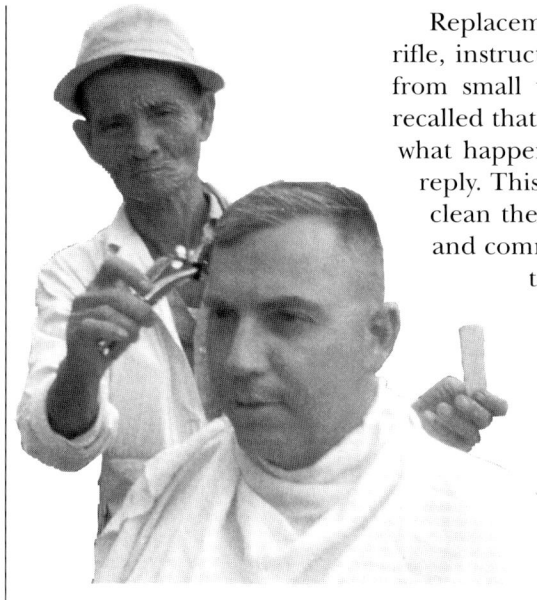

Vietnamese civilians provided services, like this 'papa-san' barber with hand clippers and single hair style — 'high and tight'. This did not encourage business from younger Marines, especially when prejudiced that Vietnamese might cut their throat if given a chance. Base workers were the most familiar Vietnamese encountered. (MCHC)

Replacement battalion was followed by familiarisation with the M16 rifle, instruction in the Marine's role in Vietnam, personal experience from small unit leaders, and something called 'civic action'. Valdez recalled that their troop handler, a veteran of Hue City, had been asked what happened in an ambush. "You die!" had been the monosyllabic reply. This same sergeant also spent extra time showing them how to clean the unfamiliar M16 and then sent them to buy paint brushes and commercial lubricant for this purpose. "If it's not clean enough to eat from, you're gonna die."

Being run through 'Asian' villages and jungle lanes in California's arid climate is an incongruity not always appreciated. Historian and 9th Marines commander in Vietnam, BrigGen Edwin H. Simmons, described one of these exercises. The demonstration "follows a simple predictable scenario… a Marine force encircles the village, forming the cordon for the cordon-and-search operation to come. A helicopter flies overhead, making a loudspeaker broadcast and dropping leaflets… One by one the VC are eliminated." All this was play-acting, without the ever-present wood smoke, cooking smells and farm animals, and the tension caused by restricted movement and visibility. For the privates it must have seemed like "a walk in the sun". Training was completed in time for Christmas and New Year's leave; then the Marines went on to first duty stations in January 1969 – with Vietnam being the destination for Privates Benotz, Valdez and Murphy. They were leaving the Age of Aquarius for the world of the Universal Soldier.

Marines served a 13-month Vietnam tour, and when ordered overseas were limited to a summer khaki uniform and an 'overnight' or 'AWOL' (for absent without leave) bag of 25 pounds. Exceptions were those who were deployed as units by ship or plane, who already had field uniforms and equipment. Departure by commercial airlines was from Travis and Norton Air Force Bases in California to Okinawa, near Japan. On Okinawa, personnel were processed through Camp Hague and then on

Sports passed the time in the rear, albeit in primitive form such as this football game at the 3rd Marine Division's Dong Ha Combat Base. This 'Dust Bowl' inter-battalion classic was played with a day's practice and won 12-0. (DOD)

to Vietnam, where they were issued with the necessary clothing and equipment at the unit level. Throughout the stay 'in country' the unit replaced items as required, sometimes by the reissue of salvaged gear. Marines left a sea bag (and a footlocker for officers and staff non-commissioned officers) in the rear with excess uniforms and belongings. In most cases these were not seen again until the Marines were 'rotated' back to the United States.

# EVERYDAY LIFE IN VIETNAM

### In the Rear with the Gear

The III Marine Amphibious Force was the senior Marine and American command in I Corps. Assigned to it were elements of the 1st and 3rd Marine Divisions, the 1st Marine Aircraft Wing and the Force Logistic Command. Allied forces in I Corps had four tasks to accomplish: defend critical bases and airfields; destroy Communist combat forces; eliminate Communist subversive infrastructure; and conduct civic action to support the government of South Vietnam. This was in an area covering 10,700 square miles, including the coastal enclaves of Phu Bai, Da Nang and Chu Lai. It encompassed a population of 2,755,800 in five provinces, six cities and 549 major villages.

Benatz, Murphy and Valdez arrived at the end of the replacement pipeline on the same commercial airline – Freedom Bird – that was used for those departing at the end of their tour. From Da Nang they were sent to Dong Ha Combat Base and 3rd Marine Division, for eventual assignment to the 9th Marines at Vandegrift Combat Base – a gruelling aircraft and truck trip to the first battalion's first company, 'Alpha 1/9'. The sprawling tent-city was hot and dirty, and smelled "like shit".

The lads were processed into the company by the executive officer, 1st Lt Lee R. Herron, and the first

Key locations in I Corps, South Vietnam (USMC)

KEY LOCATIONS IN I CORPS

Entertainment was provided by the United Services Organisation, most of which by travelling troupes of performers as opposed to the more publicised Christmas shows. In this case by University of Texas students on an improvised stage behind a metal Butler building. (MCHC)

sergeant, and then assigned to 2ndLt George M. Malone's platoon. They learned the company commander was a 'mustang' officer commissioned from the ranks, who had served in force recon and with the Vietnamese Marines. The battalion was in the field, and replacements were put on working parties to maintain the base, burning trash and latrines, and any other duties the battalion police sergeant could dream up.

Base camps had grown inside the barbed wire into fortified garrison towns. Screened Southeast Asian huts replaced tents; tarmac covered the red mud; and the food was good. General Simmons observed there were "post exchanges, chapels, clubs stratified by rank, and plentiful electricity for radios, television, refrigeration and even air conditioning". 'Little Americas' were created within base areas despite the military necessity of the deployment, a trend that became more pronounced as the war became routine. The difference between the front and the rear in terms of creature comforts was significant, and this led to some incongruous efforts to supply luxury items. Even outposts or fire support bases could have picnic-style meals helicoptered in. Shipboard living for Marines with the amphibious Special Landing Force (SLF) was an improvement too, since they were dry and well fed by the US Navy.

Marines looked forward to a six-day rest and recreation leave (R&R, also known as I&I – intercourse and intoxication) half-way through their tour, to Hawaii, Hong Kong, the Philippines, Taiwan, Japan or Australia. There was also 'In-country R&R', which sent units to China Beach in Da Nang for sleep, sun, surf and beer-bust style barbecues. "One good deal after another," commented the wags, who suspected the aviation and support personnel always lived like this.

Administrative moves within Vietnam were by motor transport. A convoy of five-ton cargo trucks churns through a bypass on Route 9 between the Dong Ha Combat Base and the Vandegrift Combat Base, a trip made daily to run supplies from division to regiment in the northern sector of I Corps. (DOD)

More urgent resupply was made by helicopters, to include water, ammunition, and rations. Normally made once a day or so, returning aircraft would also take back injured personnel and empty water containers for the next trip. These often pinpointed Marine locations and drew enemy fire. (DOD)

Replacements heard rumours about the local Vietnamese putting glass in drinks, having razors in orifices, and something called 'black syph'. The wartime personal response programme sought to instil the rapport Marines needed to win "hearts and minds" or at least prevent abuses that would drive Vietnamese civilians to the other side (an American programme and not a South Vietnamese effort). It posed the question, "So why are you here?" A scholar, Christian G. Appy, assumed that Joe, Juan, and Pat either took the war on its own terms, blocked from their minds the purpose or value of it, or gave "as little of themselves to the war as possible". Little time for introspection existed once in country and the average riflemen viewed civic action as somewhat hypocritical: "Let me win your hearts and minds or I'll burn your damn huts down." Where the 9th Marines were along the DMZ found few civilians left to deal with anyway.

# ORGANISATION FOR COMBAT

### Striking Ninth and Walking Dead

Under MajGen Raymond G. Davis, the 3rd Marine Division had been carrying out mobile operations against North Vietnamese units using superior firepower and helicopter mobility since the middle of 1968. It controlled three infantry regiments and several support or service units which together made up a complete combined-arms team, including field artillery, armour, reconnaissance, engineers, communications, motor transport, medical, maintenance and supply.

Among Davis' regiments was the 9th Marines, one of the Marine Corps 'work-horse' regiments from World War One, through World War Two and the subsequent Cold War. The 9th Marines and its battalions were deployed to Vietnam in March 1965 and remained until 1969 – "first in, first out". Along with a record of heavy combat, it had pioneered the 'county fair' approach to civic action.

Three infantry battalions and a headquarters company made up the 9th Marines Regiment. The first battalion gained notoriety as the subject of a lurid account of the burning of Cam Ne village in 1965 and as the unit Dr. Bernard B. Fall was killed with on the 'Street Without Joy'. The battalion's nickname, 'The Walking Dead', was earned through bloody fights with the North Vietnamese along the demilitarised zone under

conventional warfare conditions, notably during Operation Buffalo in 1967. These savage engagements continued through 1968 as the Marines fought along the DMZ and around Khe Sanh Combat Base.

Their grim reputation was earned, as rock-and-roll reporter Michael Herr commented, because the belief that "one Marine was better than ten Slopes saw Marine squads fed against known NVA platoons, platoons against companies, and on and on…" Herr wrote that Marine riflemen "got savaged a lot and softened a lot, their secret brutalised them and darkened them and very often it made them beautiful. It took no age, seasoning or education to make them know exactly where true violence resided." They were the killers, and 1/9's reputation, Herr felt, was the kind that "takes hold most deeply among the men of the outfit itself".

Each 1,193-man infantry battalion had four 216-man rifle companies lettered 'A'–'D' in the 1st battalion, 'E'–'H' in the 2nd battalion, and 'I'–'M' in the 3rd battalion ('J' was not used). Each battalion had its own heavy weapons support, the headquarters and service company 81mm mortars and 106mm recoilless rifles. In practice, battalions – and even companies – were used in mixed task forces.

A rifle company had a total of 210 men and six officers. The company was divided into three rifle platoons, each of about 46 men and one lieutenant; a slightly larger weapons platoon, also with one lieutenant; and a headquarters. The headquarters consisted of the captain in command of the company and those who helped him direct it in training and in battle – a lieutenant executive officer, a first sergeant, a gunnery sergeant, an armourer, a supply sergeant and administrative clerks.

**Day-to-day activities involved seeking enemy soldiers, supplies, and bunkers in sweeps of the Demilitarised Zone. Night began a constant vigil against North Vietnamese attacks after numbing daytime exertion, alternating ambushes and patrols. (DOD)**

**Marine Rifle Company Organization (USMC)**

RIFLE COMPANY (RIFLE CO)
INFANTRY BATTALION

T/O M-1013 Rev 2 6Jun67
T/E M-1013

<u>Primary Mission:</u> To locate, close with and destroy the enemy by fire and maneuver or to repel his assault by fire and close combat.

| | RIFLE CO | | | |
| --- | --- | --- | --- | --- |
| | USMC | | USN | |
| | OFF | ENL | OFF | ENL |
| | 6 | 210 | 0 | 0 |

| CO HQ | WPNS PLAT | RIFLE PLAT |
| --- | --- | --- |
| 2-7    0-0 | 1-65    0-0 | 1-46    0-0 |

<u>Major Items of Equipment:</u>

6 Machine Gun 7.62mm M60
9 Grenade Launcher, M79
6 Rocket Launcher, 3.5, M20A1
3 Infantry Mortar 60 mm

Support for the three rifle platoons was from a weapons platoon which had three sections besides its small headquarters group (in which were the platoon leader, platoon sergeant and a small number of others). The three sections were: the 60mm mortar section, with three M19 mortars and crews; an M60 machine-gun section, with three two-gun squads and crews; and an assault section of three squads of two teams each (by 1969 the M20 rocket launcher had usually been replaced by the M72 light-anti-armour-weapon, or LAAW).

The three rifle platoons were each led by a lieutenant who had a staff sergeant as his second-in-command. In each platoon there were three rifle squads and a small command group – the platoon leader, a platoon sergeant, a right guide, a radio operator and a medical corpsman. Each of the rifle squads was led by a sergeant, and these 14 men usually had among them 13 M16 rifles and one M79 grenade-launcher. All these Marines carried a number of hand-grenades and most had bayonets to put on their rifles; some had knives. A fire-team of four men was the basic unit, with a team leader (the senior man), an automatic rifleman (next senior and designated to use automatic fire) and two riflemen (a scout and an assistant automatic rifleman). The actual number of personnel present was often below that authorised, with the ebb and flow of manpower demands.

ABOVE **Commanding the 3d Marine Division from 1968 – 1969 was MajGen Raymond G. Davis. A veteran of World War Two and Korea, where he earned a Medal of Honor, Davis used his battalions to search and destroy the enemy forces in I Corps. (DOD)**

**The 9th Marine Regiment was commanded by Col Robert H. Barrow, another veteran of World War Two and Korea, and later Commandant of the Marine Corps. He took three battalions in the most successful regimental-size operation of the war, code-named 'Dewey Canyon'. (DOD)**

# CAMPAIGN LIFE IN VIETNAM

### In the Boondocks

While a member of a Corps that stressed air-ground task forces and combined arms teams, it was still the infantry that bore the brunt of the daily burden of combat, in conditions that placed them on a relatively equitable footing in a fire-fight with a deadly enemy; after a while in the bush, their attitudes and mannerisms changed from the more civilised ones of the rear echelon.

General Simmons wrote that the realities of war for Marine riflemen were "heat, wetness, malaria, leeches, repetitive patrols, ambushes, sapper attacks and antipersonnel mines". The infantry's experience of combat was qualitatively and quantitatively different to that of support and service personnel, even though their modern warfare was very much a team effort. Newsman George Casey reported that the average Grunt accepted "the facts of rotting wrist watch bands, a 'Dear John' letter, reconstituted milk, canned meat, three salt tablets a day, last choice of C rations and warm beer". One Marine reconnaissance unit veteran commented that at least he rotated patrols and had time in between to rest and relax before going out again; but in the infantry "you went out and stayed out".

The return to Vandegrift base of the rest of Alpha Company did not ease the burden on new replacements who were generally overlooked. First platoon had a lot of Southerners, as well as some Midwesterners, none of whom were very forthcoming. Squad leader Sgt Leroy Black, of Detroit, Michigan, turned Benotz, Valdez and Murphy over to their fire-team leader, Cpl Mike Smith of Topeka, Kansas. The taciturn Black was on a second combat tour, while Smith was six months into his assignment. What Smith and Black thought was guarded by realities they faced.

One day the platoon guide took Valdez, Benotz and Murphy to pick up rations and ammunition. Valdez asked: "Sarge, what gives with the squad? No-one will talk to us." Perhaps because Valdez was the quietest of the three, the sergeant responded: "It's like this: they knew the guys you replaced and they don't know you. You might foul up and get them killed or they'll foul up and get you killed – so they won't get too close."

Unknown to our 'chosen' men, but of major importance all the same, in January 1969 the III MAF and I Corps commands were concerned about expanded enemy activity in the Annamite mountain range, where Communist forces from Laos were moving along Routes 922 in Laos and 548 in South Vietnam, leading to Hue, Da Nang and the populated coastal plain. Troop and supply concentrations were evident in Base Area 611 astride the international border. Recent increases

Alpha Company, 9th Marines was led by 1stLt Wesley L. Fox during Operation 'Dewey Canyon'. Lieutenant Fox fought his company against an enemy bunker complex and earned a Medal of Honor. The fire team in this narrative was in Alpha's first platoon. (DOD)

Into the valley! Lead elements of the 9th Marines kicked off Operation 'Dewey Canyon' with helicopter assaults in the Da Krong Valley to establish fire support bases. Initial landing sites were 'prepped' with artillery fire and air strikes. (DOD)

in anti-aircraft defences had indicated that the NVA had something to protect. This was to be the origin of the operation codenamed 'Dewey Canyon' that took 'our men' into combat for the first time.

Sergeant Black simplified tactics for old and new 'hands' as they prepared to move to the field: "Keep your head out of your ass and pay attention to what is going on. Keep your eyes on your team leaders and me – you watch me and follow what I do pronto. When I get down, you drop; when I shoot, you open fire; when I run, you haul ass – no more no less. If you new guys screw up, you won't last – forget all that John Wayne stuff over here. If you shoot, shoot to kill, stay alert and you might stay alive – if not, sorry about that."

# UNIFORMS, EQUIPMENT, WEAPONS

## Tools of the Trade

### Appearance

Though American combat uniforms in Vietnam looked the same, the alert observer can detect differences between soldiers and Marines. This is explained by procurement, supply practices and local conditions, and varied according to individual or unit preference, authorisation of weapons, unit missions and the type of organisation (combat, support or service). Once overseas, the Marines were often far from their depots in the United States and had to adapt to whatever materiel was at hand. Marines also had an affectation for 'salty' clothing and equipment – they preferred older items to newer things to convey an image of experience. The supply system was not consistent enough to allow completely uniform appearance, so despite regulation, variety flourished.

Individual or 'tribal' markings were seen in beards, bracelets, necklaces, helmet graffiti, tattoos and even flags. The longer a unit remained in the field, the 'grungier' they would look, as uniforms and equipment took on the faded hue of the dust in the local area. Personnel displayed a characteristic 'farmer's' tan on their faces, necks and arms after a few days exposed to the sun. Grooming varied according to where a person was and how close to a barber shop. Uniform regulations required a haircut to start from zero at the normal hairline to no more than three inches on top. For practical purposes, American Marines did not have sideburns or long hair down the back of the neck. Moustaches

Touch down and go! A CH46 Sea Knight of MAG-36 lifts-off after landing a squad of riflemen in a landing zone adjacent to the site of a proposed fire support base to prepare it for follow-on forces, including artillery and supplies. (DOD)

were allowed, but not beards, but lack of water sometimes prevented shaving, and 'field' beards resulted.

**Insignia and Markings**

During the war the Marines had 12 enlisted grades and 14 grades of warrant and commissioned officers. The rank insignia was a metal or synthetic pin-on type, with black chevrons for enlisted grades and bright silver or gold for officers. Insignia was worn on both collars, if worn at all in the field. Enlisted rank was at an angle to the front edge of the collar and officer rank was worn centred and parallel to the front collar edge.

Individuals marked personal uniform items with their name at designated places, generally with a stamp or stencil in black block letters. More obvious name placement was used overseas – above the left jacket pocket and across the back of the jacket. Mistakes or changes were blotted out with ink, which made for messy uniforms.

Identification tags were aluminium with an individual's name, service number, religion and blood type. Issued in pairs, they were worn around the neck on a chain or attached to the laces of boots. In case of death, one was taken for reporting and the other was left with the body for identification. Tape or rubber sheaths were used to silence the tags.

Groundwork included clearing trees and vegetation to allow helicopters to bring in engineer support and material to rapidly bring the fire support base into operation. The initial landing zones were levelled with hand tools. (DOD)

The Marines emphasised service rather than unit loyalty. To enhance this, no insignia was worn except the corps emblem. The 1954 branch-of-service 'Eagle, Globe and Anchor' emblem was found on the cap and shirt. Most utility jackets were issued unmarked with a service emblem, and the individual used heat transfer or stencils to apply them on the left pocket 'over the heart'. With unit replacement of clothing in Vietnam, these USMC transfers were not always available.

## Headgear

The distinctive sage green utility 'cover' was the common headgear. It was an olive-green sateen M58 version of a World War Two design. Rank insignia was fixed at the crown when not visible elsewhere. When not in use, the utility cover was folded and kept in a helmet liner or trouser-leg pocket. During the Vietnam era, tropical ('boonie' or 'bush') hats of all types were available in olive-green and camouflage patterns. Versions were manufactured for the various hot weather uniforms, since the hat provided full cover of the head and neck. Issued or traded on the local economy, they were often worn instead of the utility cover. Sweat rags of olive-green towels or cravat bandages were worn around the neck or head. A sweat band could also be made from the strap and safety pin of cloth ammunition bandoleers.

## Utility Uniforms

Marines had some options in field clothing. There were the standard M62 sateen utilities, jungle utilities from 1966 and camouflage utilities from 1968. The first pattern jungle utilities were designed for the special

**A CH53 Sea Stallion lands at Fire Support Base Razor amidst smoke and fog of war. Infantrymen of the 9th Marines and artillerymen of the 12th Marines take a break for Sunday services by a navy chaplain in a mortar position chapel made of ammo and ration boxes. (DOD)**

forces, based on World War Two army airborne clothing. The olive-green uniform was durable and fast drying, several modifications evolved, but the basic design remained the same.

The camouflage version of the jungle utilities was in the four-colour US Army Engineer Research Development Laboratory leaf pattern. The jacket and trousers were camouflage, 100% cotton, wind resistant rip-stop cotton poplin (Class 2). The jacket had four pleated bellows pockets and was worn outside the trousers. The trousers had four pockets on the hips and two expanding pockets on the trouser legs. Buttons were plastic and allowed closure at the collar and wrist. Although popular, it suffered the problem of most camouflage uniforms: it was great when you were standing still but drew attention when you moved. Eventually the camouflage uniform was adapted to a distinct III MAF uniform.

Supplementary clothing was held by the unit and used as needed. Some items were commonplace, such as M65 field jackets, raincoats and various other waterproof clothing. Supplemental uniform items allowed for a certain amount of mixing and matching, hence the label 'raggedy-ass' Marines, given them by more consistent formations.

Issue olive-green underwear was worn, if any was worn at all, in the field. A standard khaki web belt with an open face brass buckle was also used. Worn with all uniforms, the web belt remained popular, as it was one of the Marine Corps' unique items. The web belt doubled as a cargo strap to secure ammunition boxes or equipment. Extra belts were used, such as 'jungle' belts made from suspender straps and a variety of captured NVA belts.

PFC Robert T. Ikner displays blocks of explosives dropped by North Vietnamese Army troops during s sapper attack on a fire support base. He had ducked into his fighting position to reload his rifle when he heard the enemy soldiers on top of the bunker with the charges and shot them in the act. (DOD)

### Footwear

The green nylon and black leather tropical combat boots were preferred in Vietnam and were worn as available, again later in Marine units than in army units. Black or olive-green socks were worn – either all-cotton, all-wool or blends with nylon. In the field a spare pair of socks was kept in a plastic radio-battery bag to rotate when one pair was wet. Boot socks were also used to carry ration cans tied to the back or side of the pack and to pad or silence other items of equipment. Trousers were worn bloused around the boot top with 'blousing garters' rather than being tucked into the boot top in the army style.

### Body Armour

An M1 steel helmet with a separate fibre liner was adopted in 1941 and was in service with the Marines the following year. This helmet, with a single chin strap, was used in Vietnam. It was issued to all hands, and the standard infantry practice was to wear it constantly. In 1962 a defence department standard, leaf pattern, canvas helmet cover with reversible green and brown sides was adopted, and this served through the Vietnam War. It soon faded with use, far beyond that of army units. To hold foliage in place on the helmets, bands made of rubber inner-tube material or army-issue olive-green elastic were used.

The use of body armour varied with the task at hand and was worn by infantry units in Vietnam. Modern body armour was introduced to Marines in Korea with the M51 and M55 protective body armour – the 'flak' jacket, with its angular plates, was characteristic, although army M69 versions were also used in Vietnam. Metal eyelets on the waist of the jacket allowed equipment to be hooked onto it, so the cartridge belt and harness could be dispensed with. Later models had two pockets added to the lower front. They were designed, like the helmet, to protect from fragmentation and were not bullet-proof. Body armour was most suitable for static positions and gun crews, but it became a permanent part of the equipment issue for a number of reasons and was worn over an undershirt or bare skin in hot weather.

Both the helmet and the body armour were described by one 9th Marines company commander as "hard to live with and sometimes impossible to live without". The already overloaded Marine sacrificed mobility for the sake of protection. Although wear was mandatory, the 2nd Battalion, 9th Marines left its helmets and flak jackets behind when it operated in Laos during Dewey Canyon.

Graffiti on helmets and flak jackets included the nine-digit social security number, the older, seven-digit, service number or the four-digit 'military occupational specialty' (MOS) number – 0311 for infantryman, 0321 for machine-gunner, 0352 for anti-tank man and so on. These numbers helped identify individual equipment, even though this was not approved. A Marine's surname initial and last four numbers of his social security number would be used to identify his web gear – for example, 'M-1488' – a unique method of personalisation when the use of a name would be frowned upon. It also became a means of expressing identity or opinion. Names of home states, cities, girlfriends and nicknames all made this graffiti the ground-pounder's equivalent of aircraft nose art. It was a practice suppressed in the rear areas and was the bane of the junior officer and the non-commissioned officer.

Communist sharpshooters waged a contest with Marines as they moved out of exposed positions. In one-for-two, PFC Ronnie S. Tucker and PFC Robert M. Moxley examine their helmets which were both hit by the same enemy round. Neither was injured in this close call. (DOD)

## Equipment

The Marine Corps M1941 Pack and Individual Combat Equipment served in World War Two and the Korean War. Equipment with a 1941 date stamp was still being issued in Vietnam, but most had been replaced by army M1956 Load Carrying Equipment (LCE) in olive-green cotton canvas and the later M1967 Modernized Load Carrying Equipment (MLCE or LC1) in olive-green nylon.

Army and Marine Corps gear was intermingled throughout, since equipment was not often issued in matched or complete sets. For the purposes of this book, basic allocations will be considered; model and year designations refer to generations of equipment rather than formal patterns, date of issue or manufacture.

The term 'Grunt' meant the same for American Marines as 'Marius

Mule' had for Roman legionnaires. Despite the desired body-to-load weight ratio of three-to-one, the typical Marine carried in excess of the recommended 50-pound maximum, usually more like 80–100 pounds. This reflected the belief that if you did not carry something, then you did not have it, as well as limitations of helicopter and vehicle transport once a unit was on foot.

A fighting load in Vietnam consisted of: a cartridge belt; a field dressing and first aid kit (the M56 utility pouch held a standard field dressing or cigarettes, compass, whistles etc); two or more M56 universal pouches, each with three M16 rifle magazines; and two or more M62 canteens, with M56 cases worn on the belt or pack. A bayonet or knife and an M16 bipod carrying case/cleaning kit would also be on the belt. This 'war belt' was suspended from a pair of M41 belt suspender straps, but the M56 suspenders were superior and preferred by all who used them.

A subsistence load might consist of as little as the M56 combat field pack (or 'ass pack') and a case from an M17A1 field protective mask or demolitions and claymore bags for a 'day trip'. The M41 haversack held the minimum possible that a Marine needed to live for a extended period. (This was a matter of experience, with new men enduring the maximum load and the veteran shedding as much weight as possible.) It generally included a poncho, rations (sometimes stacked in a boot sock and hung off the pack or harness), toiletries and a folding shovel. The poncho deserves mention as a combination groundsheet, tent and blanket for most nights in the field.

Additional items depended upon terrain and weather, and included poncho liners, rain suits, field jackets, sleeping shirts, spare socks and a 'rubber bitch' air mattress. Personal touches were seen in bush hats, tiger-stripe shorts, sun glasses, reading material, knick-knacks, extra knives and pistols. Field modifications included taped or rubber cushioned identification tags, metal canteens covered with boot socks to

ABOVE **An American sniper team indicates the enemy has shown himself long enough to obtain a shot with an M40 sniper rifle. Cat-and-mouse type engagements characterised the minor tactics of Dewey Canyon's first phase. (DOD)**

prevent noise, and yards of black electrician's or green ordnance tape to cushion, fasten or cover equipment. The indigenous ARVN rucksack and the US Army tropical rucksack were popular, and were used when available. Even captured Chinese-made packs were used, and were preferred to the M41 haversack because of their external pockets. A 9th Marines battalion commander, LtCol Elliot R. Laine Jr., observed that he used the M41 pack first, and when it did not carry the load he tried ARVN and even NVA packs. Finally he settled on the tropical rucksack which he got for his battalion through a barter with army units.

Officers and non-commissioned officers carried the same clothing and equipment as enlisted Marines. Differences included the pistol belt, a black leather holster, a pistol magazine pouch holding two magazines, canteens, a first aid kit and 'H' harness or belt suspender straps. A 'tanker' pistol shoulder holster in black leather was sometimes used; it was designed to be worn with two straps, one around the chest and the other over the shoulder. Compasses, strobe lights and signal mirrors were carried in either pouches or pockets, often tied to the belt with an 'idiot cord' made from a boot lace or parachute suspension line. A watch might be worn with the wrist strap through a button hole of the shirt or breast pocket. Leaders of small units had an assortment of maps, notebooks, radio code sheets and tactical book-keeping materiel necessary for their tasks. As combat became more direct, front-line leaders adapted the uniform and look of the rifleman to avoid standing out. This was hard to do when followed by one or more radio operators and the headquarters element of even the smallest sized unit.

## Weapons and Radios

In most situations, units went armed to the teeth, with machine-guns and mortars, because of the need to hold their own without immediate support; they had been trained to 'move to shoot and shoot to move' with organic weapons. The general-purpose weapon was the M16A1 rifle, but sometimes pistols and even shotguns were useful. The M16 was an innovative design using aircraft-industry manufacturing techniques and material. It was fielded in Vietnam with problems in ammunition, training, and maintenance materials (there were no provision with the rifle to carry cleaning tools), but these had been overcome by 1969.

A battalion weapons coach explained to some replacements the difference between range qualification and fire-fights. He was asked how often they were likely to be surprised when in the field? "Let's just say, too often. You will find yourself pinned down, unable to return fire, or firing and manoeuvring for all you're worth." Sight alignment and trigger squeeze were hardly relevant: "He who shoots and kills first is going to win. Shoot low. Push the muzzle down. You can see where the first shot hits. You can get him with a ricochet." These were the instructions given Murphy, Valdez and Benotz as they sighted their M16s on some

LEFT, BELOW **Battles are won by manoeuvre as well as fire, with 1st Battalion, 9th Marines moving out from Fire Support Base Erskine just north of the Ashau Valley. The infantry carried everything to fight and survive, while those who remained benefited from a static assignment. (DOD)**

M16 Rifle Schematic — The 'Sweet Sixteen' was adapted for use in Vietnam and later became the standard American service rifle. Basic marksmanship training was conducted with the earlier 7.62mm M14 rifle. (USMC)

55-gallon drums at the combat base perimeter. Don't shoot once and look. "Keep firing until the gook goes down, and fire insurance rounds to make him bounce."

Squad-level M79 grenade-launchers were used to knock out direct-fire weapons so riflemen did not have to become exposed in order to throw hand-grenades or to fire rifles at an enemy position. Grenade-launchers are very handy weapons, but are slow to reload. Sgt Black carried his squad's grenade-launcher in order to ensure its use where needed.

Officers, non-commissioned officers, grenadiers and machine-gunners were armed with the venerable M1911A1 automatic pistol, with its distinctive kick and its large, slow projectile which was designed to knock the enemy down with a body-hit. These pistols were from stocks that had last been procured in 1945. It was considered a back-up weapon, and the feeling was that a rifle was preferable in a real fire-fight.

Hand grenades carried included M26 or M67 fragmentation, M18 smoke and M15 white phosphorus types. They were used to blast, burn or smoke the enemy out of his hole or to break up rushes at close range. Grenades could be a problem if left hanging off the webbing, including the M56 magazine pouches designed to carry them this way. The spoons would bend and break after a time allowing the grenade to drop off ('scoring your own goal'). If carried in fibreboard storage tubes or grenade pouches, they were hard to get at in a fire-fight. Other useful weapons were the command detonated M18 Claymore mine, the M49 trip flare and the M133/135 demolition 'satchel' charges.

For 'close combat', each rifle came with a bayonet knife and scabbard – the M7 for an M16 – and these served as general purpose knives as well. Marines had a 12-inch all-steel, Bowie-style 'Ka-Bar' knife that was issued to everyone who carried a pistol, including machine-gunners, grenadiers, corpsmen, officers and staff noncommissioned officers. Most wore them on the left side of their pistol belt. The fighting knife

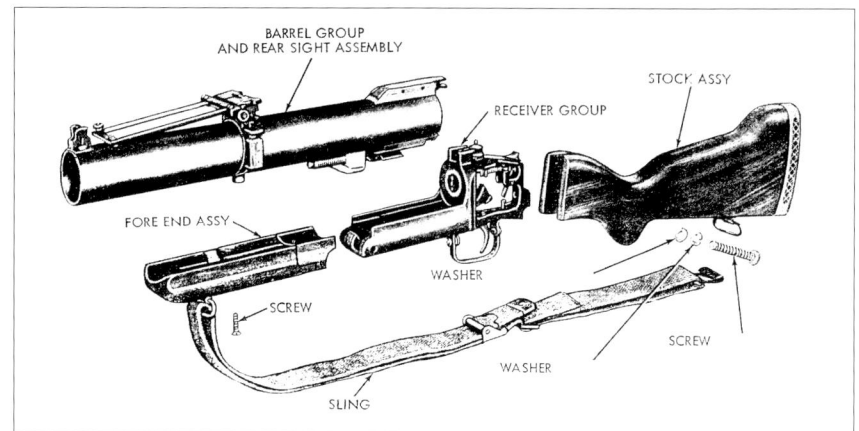

**M79 Grenade Launcher Schematic** — The 'Blooper' was carried by the squad's grenadier for indirect fire beyond hand grenade range. Handy, if slow to reload, it had a 5 yard fragmentation range. (DOD)

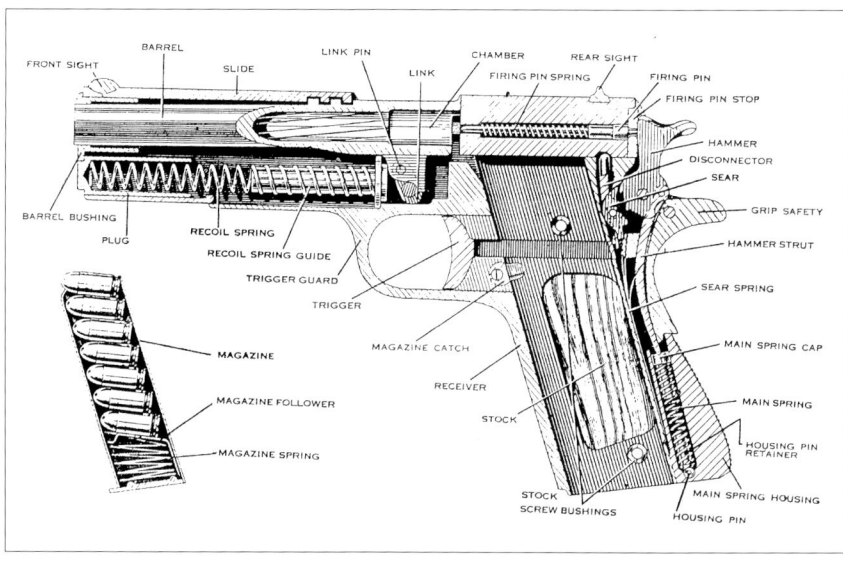

**M1911 Pistol Schematic** – The 'Colt Forty-Five' had been the standard pistol in Marine infantry units since World War One. It was carried by all those not armed with the service rifle. (DOD)

was used more as a general purpose tool, as everything 'from a hammer to a pry bar'. The 'E tool' folding shovel was a more practical hand-to-hand weapon.

Voice commands and hand and arms signals were common at squad level. Other communications methods included flares, smoke, blinker lamps, flags, air-panels and runners. The battalion provided radios and operators down to company level, while platoons had to train their own personnel to operate and carry the radio with the platoon leader. Communications equipment included AN/PRC25 very high frequency radios and TA1 telephones for talking with the rear, within a unit, or to aircraft or artillery firing in support. A sophisticated system of communications for their control was present from the highest to the lowest level.

The III MAF commander LtGen Herman Nickerson Jr. wrote that the troop commanders had to "effectively employ weapons that span the spectrum from 60mm mortars and eight-inch naval guns to 2,000-pound bombs. In each confrontation with the enemy, he must determine rapidly what supporting arms are available, which are the best weapons to employ, and then coordinate their use with all agencies involved." Instructions to his subordinates from squad leader to division commander were: "We have the resources. We must use them properly. Those of us who do not use our artillery, air, naval gunfire in seizing objectives are not professional."

**M60 Machine Gun Schematic — The 'Pig' was found in the weapons platoon of the rifle company. It was often carried and used at the platoon or squad level to the cry of 'guns up!' (DOD)**

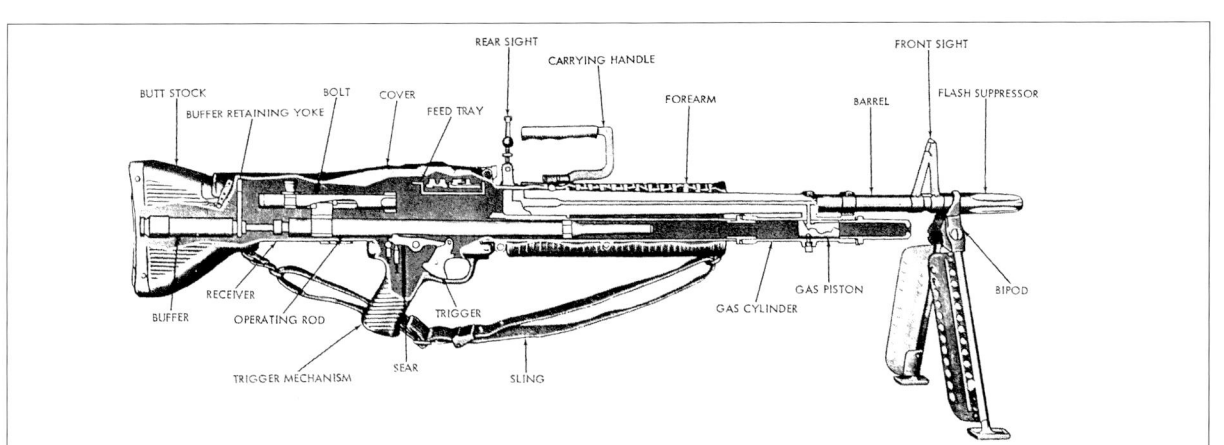

# SUPPLY AND RESUPPLY

### Water, rations and ammo

One Vietnam veteran recalled that resupply of essentials to frontline units was "frequent and reliable". While regiments and battalions had sections that specialised in furnishing the 10 classes of supplies, at the lower level this was the commanders' responsibility, with help from the gunnery sergeant at the company level and the right guide within a platoon. Both the company gunny and the platoon guide were the second senior noncommissioned officer of their units. Their major concern was provision of rations, water, batteries and ammunition, and replacement clothing or ordnance items. They accomplished this with

Into the boondocks with Alpha Company as Cpl Smith's men learn what it means to be foot mobile in all terrains and weather. The pickaxe was 'borrowed' from the engineers on leaving the fire support base to supplement individual entrenching tools. (DOD)

Management of violence was the task of infantry command groups distinguished by maps and radios. Increased enemy resistance required the use of supporting arms, either artillery or air power. Bulky command elements also had to protect themselves from close-in attack. (USNI)

working parties drawn from subordinates, and organised carrying parties and landing zones during operations.

The basic allowance of ammunition included 350–420 rounds of 5.56mm rifle ammunition in magazines and cloth bandoleers. There were 21 rounds of .45 calibre ACP ammunition for each pistol and 800 rounds of linked 7.62mm ammunition per machine-gun. Grenade-launcher 40mm rounds were carried in claymore and demolition bags or in special bandoleers and vests. Crew served weapon ammunition was passed out to spread the load. This might include one or two M72 anti-tank rocket rounds, one or two 81mm mortar rounds, between one and three 60mm mortar rounds, illumination flares ('pop-ups') and machine-gun ammunition in boxes or belts. The M60 ammunition was carried in the box, bandoleer or slung across the chest, depending on the situation and unit control. Slung ammunition was easier to carry but was subject to wastage or dirt and damage. Grenades, spare barrel bags and radio batteries completed the load wherever they could be toted.

Water was as important as ammunition and medical evacuation in the infantry leader's priorities. It was delivered in green metal or black plastic 'Jerry' cans to static defensive positions and landing zones, or obtained from local streams and purified with issue halazone or iodine tablets, to be carried in individual canteens. The total number of canteens carried depended on the conditions and early in the war it was found that one canteen was not enough. Water discipline and the use of salt tablets were stressed as rifleman settled for tepid, adulterated and often murky refreshment.

Meals served at base mess halls or from insulated 'vat cans' brought to the field were known as A and B Rations. The field ration was the

Meal, Combat Individual or 'C-Rat'. These were issued 12 meals to a case. A Marine would be issued a whole case (22 pounds) to have a four-day supply. He opened the individual boxes, discarded things he did not like or could not trade and packed the rest where he could in his pack or belt. In each case was a supply of can openers, the P38 or 'John Wayne' that came with a hole that allowed it to be worn on the dog-tag chain or on the helmet band. A steady diet of three meals a day was about 3,300 calories, but because of the terrain and the weather, fruit, crackers and one main or heavy meal a day was usually about all most would eat, more like 1,100 calories a day, resulting in weight loss (cold weather improved appetites).

A meal box contained a white plastic spoon (retained in a helmet band or pocket for later use), an accessory pack, a 'B' unit (crackers, candy, cheese) and the main meal (or 'heavy'). Menus included ham and eggs, spiced beef, ham and lima beans, pork steak, meat balls and beans, franks and beans, chicken and noodles, turkey load and beef slices. Cigarettes were in the rations in packs of four and were useful for trading purposes. Hot coffee was also popular for an early morning or late evening 'jump start' drink. Efforts to improve the main meal were seen in the use of hot sauce, worcestershire sauce and peppers or wild onions. In most instances rations were eaten cold, since there was neither the time nor the interest to heat with trioxane fuel bars or a pinch of C4 plastic explosives. Another speculation was that if you mixed cold and hot meals you suffered constipation or diarrhoea.

A mortar crew prepares to fire the company commander's 'hip-pocket' artillery, the 60mm mortar. This was often the quickest supporting arm to bring into play and could be carried by the rifle companies. (DOD)

To reduce rations' weight, special dehydrated patrol rations were developed by the army, called the Ration, Long Range Patrol (LRP). These were packed in cloth-wrapped plastic and foil envelopes that required water to prepare. Menus included chili, spaghetti, chicken stew and beef stew. An accessory pack, candy, a cereal bar and cocoa were standard additions. A package would be opened, water and seasoning would be added, then it was folded and held down with a rubber band and carried in a pocket, where it marinated until consumed. They were light: three days of LRP rations weighed eight pounds compared to the C rations' 18 pounds. 'Lurps', as they were known, were just as dull as C rations to eat and were not fit as long term supplies. In the field, ration issue was by unit. This involved cased meals being moved from battalion to company to platoon to squad. The company gunnery sergeant, platoon guide or squad leader would up-end a carton so that the contents were hidden and meals would be issued at random. An experienced small unit leader would mix the order of the meals up in the case, since after a while a Marine knew what meal was located in the case by position. Rubbish was repacked in the meal box and returned to the case to be sent back or left.

For Operation Dewey Canyon each rifleman was issued four days of food, an LRP for emergencies, four canteens of water and twice the normal load of ammunition and batteries. For the seven weeks of the operation resupply and casualty replacement were difficult – units went on short rations or no provisions for a day or two. Ammunition, water and batteries were a constant resupply problem. It was hard to replenish rifle companies without stopping their movement because finding them from the air was impossible. Once supplies had been delivered, a detail of up to platoon-size had to remain to return cargo nets and empty water containers. Later, supplies were delivered on wooden pallets or in canvas bundles slung from disposable steel cable that could be left behind. The five-gallon plastic water containers were not enough to supply the volume required and they often leaked. Artillery canisters were used, each holding about 13 gallons of water. Beer or sodas were even obtainable at one per man, but were extraordinary enough to be memorable.

# MEDEVAC

### Shot at and hit

"Combat casualties frequently appear in overwhelming numbers, suffer from multiple fragment wounds and often have waited hours for evacuation and treatment. Add to that austere facilities, equipment and supplies, an echeloned treatment chain, and combat conditions, and it is clear that wartime military medicine presents unique demands," testified a US Navy doctor to the US Senate Committee on Armed Services. This is an accurate description of Vietnam medical conditions.

During the war 14,809 Marines were killed, died or were missing; another 88,635 were wounded. The majority (78%) of those killed were 21 years old or younger in the ranks from private-first-class to corporal (lieutenant to captain for officers). In contrast to World War Two and Korea, small arms fire accounted for 51% of deaths and 16% of wounds to personnel; artillery and mortar fragments were the next most common cause, with 36% of deaths and

A 155mm howitzer fires-for-effect to deliver a big punch to the enemy in all weather and all hours. Conditions at hill-top battery positions remained primitive throughout a temporary stay for the duration of the operation. (DOD)

# OSPREY

## MILITARY JOURNAL

THE INTERNATIONAL REVIEW OF MILITARY HISTORY

King Richard III: Villain or Victim?

Mosby snatches a Yankee General

US Marines on the Western Front 1918

Plus Reviews of Books, Games and Model Kits

Fascinating articles on military history from antiquity to modern times

THE SAMURAI

WARRIOR SERIES

BRITISH TOMMY 1914-18

WEAPONS · ARMOUR · TACTICS

The Wars of the Roses

MEN-AT-ARMS

THE KING'S GERMAN LEGION (2) 1812-1816

ARMIES OF THE PHARAOHS

CAMPAIGN

SLAUGHTER AT THE BARRICADES

NAGASHINO 1575

STEPHEN TURNBULL

TEXAS RANGERS

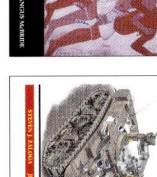

NEW VANGUARD

M3 & M5 STUART LIGHT TANK 1940-1945

French Aces of World War 2

*OSPREY MILITARY JOURNAL* - From the world's leading publisher of illustrated military history. Bi monthly (six issues per year) 64 pages per issue fully illustrated in Osprey's unique style with artwork, maps, charts and photos. Fascinating articles on military history from ancient times to the present day and expert guidance for enthusiasts.

☐ (Please tick) Please send me full details of the Osprey Military Journal, with no obligation to subscribe.

☐ (Please tick) Please send me regular information about Osprey books.

Primary area of interest:

☐ History (Please tick)  ☐ Aviation (Please tick)  ☐ Modelling (Please tick)  ☐ Wargaming (Please tick)

☐ other....................

Title/Rank (*BLOCK LETTERS PLEASE*) First name: _____

Last name: _____

Address: _____

_____

_____

Postcode/Zip: _____  Country: _____

Tel: _____  E-mail address: _____

The publisher may wish to pass on your details to carefully selected companies with publications or products of possible interest to you. If you prefer not to receive such offers, please tick here ☐

## MAIL/FAX THIS CARD TO

### In **UK, Europe and other countries**

Osprey Direct
PO Box 140
Wellingborough
Northants
NN8 4ZA
UK

Tel +44 (0)1933 443863
Fax +44 (0)1933 443849
or E-mail info@ospreydirect.co.uk

### In **USA and Canada**

Osprey Direct USA
PO Box 130
Sterling Heights
MI 48311-0130
USA

Tel (810) 795-2763
Fax (810) 795-4266
or E-mail info@ospreydirectusa.com

Visit Osprey at www.ospreypublishing.com

65% of wounds; mines, booby-traps and other methods accounted for 13% of the fatalities and 19% of injuries (mine and booby-traps were not common in Dewey Canyon's remote location). Mortal wounds to the head, torso and groin were most common, while most nonfatal injuries were in the limbs. This provided the medical logic behind digging foxholes and wearing body armour. One company commander during Dewey Canyon observed that many Marines were killed even though they were wearing flak jackets. "They were ambushed at close range with small arms fire which penetrated their body armor."

Because of the nature of the war, Marines had an unspoken conviction that wounded or dead should not be left behind, and they took great risks to ensure this, even suffering more casualties in the process. The Communists recognised this and would often try to trap the wounded near their fighting positions to limit the use of heavy weapons and draw in more Marines to rescue their mates.

In battle, an individual was expected to provide self-aid if injured; his fellow Marines were expected to keep to the task at hand and not care for the wounded. Marines carried one or two battle dressings for their own use, as well as a 'jungle' first aid kit with some 10 other items for use if sick or injured. The drill was to always first use the injured man's own dressing, not your own.

US Navy medical corpsmen at platoon and company levels provided follow-up and life saving treatment, often with great skill under trying conditions and at great personal risk. Corpsmen carried a 'Unit One' medical instrument and supply set and stocked it with as much extra medical supplies as experience and stamina allowed them to carry. A bit older and more educated than the average Marine, the corpsman's nickname 'Doc' was one of respect and hope against needing his attention. Away from combat, corpsmen supervised routine sick calls, medications and sanitation within the platoon and company area. General concerns were malaria prevention, jungle rot and scratches that led to infections because of lack of soap and water.

The use of helicopters for rapid medical evacuation was an enduring image of the Vietnam War, and saved lives that would otherwise have been lost. The decision to evacuate was made by the unit commander, working with his corpsman and based upon the tactical situation. The movement of casualties paralleled the route supplies and replacements were taking, and was aided by platoon guides and the company gunnery sergeant.

During Dewey Canyon, medical evacuation and replacement of personnel was limited due to the cross-country movement to fire support bases

**'Snake-and-nape', high explosive and fire bombs, are delivered by an F4 Phantom dropping a 500 pound MK82 Snakeye bomb on Communist trenches in the tree line. The fins of the bomb open to delay its flight until the aircraft is clear of fragments. At this point the infantry would also hit the deck. (USNI)**

**Heads up Charlie! A former North Vietnamese soldier demonstrates with an AK47 assault rifle how to fire at low-flying US aircraft. He was a 'Hoi-Chanh' who rallied to the side of the Republic of Vietnam, which explains why the rifle is on 'safe'.**

and because of poor flying weather. Casualty evacuation was risky, and the wounded and dead had to remain with the units until evacuation could be arranged, despite the efforts of helicopter crews to get them out – a morale lowering plight for those on the ground. In a number of cases, hoists were used because of the lack of landing sites. Often less serious casualties reduced unit effectiveness in the move southward, until personnel already in the field could be shifted around. One company officer wrote: "If a fire-team sustains only two casualties, or even one in some instances, it simply ceases to exist as a tactical or maneuver unit." This vital cornerstone of the tactical structure had to be reorganised whenever this happened, reducing squads to two fire-teams rather than the normal three.

# IN BATTLE

## Operation Dewey Canyon

Air and ground reconnaissance tracked the Communist build-up in Base Area 611 and this information was expanded by other agencies available to the 3rd Marine Division. General Davis recalled that 40% of his area was secured by combat forces and the rest was "covered by reconnaissance" with patrols from 3rd Force Reconnaissance Company and 3rd Reconnaissance Battalion. These patrols were used to make contact with the enemy, who were then exploited by a rapid build-up of infantry or air and artillery fire. This was the type of attack called for to disrupt Base Area 611, using a force built around the 9th Marine Regiment led by Colonel Robert H. Barrow.

Elements of two NVA infantry regiments, an artillery regiment and service-engineer-transportation troops were discovered. With these, the enemy was able to reinforce points under attack, counter-attack with small units making considerable use of crew-served weapons, and hit fire support bases. General Nickerson observed that in the North Vietnamese "…we confront a dedicated foot soldier, but a soldier lacking in supporting arms. The test of a North Vietnamese commander then is to counter our overwhelming firepower. And he doesn't mind losing troops to gain his limited objectives." The 9th Marines' commander felt that the NVA was "well organised and formidable" and abundantly supplied and equipped in terrain that helped his defence. "He was strong and he fought hard," Barrow concluded.

To go after the North Vietnamese, the Marines had to operate 20–30 air-miles beyond other allied bases – far from naval gunfire, resupply by road and reinforcement. The battle area was in a remote corner of the mountain highlands, and included the converging valleys of the Da Krong and Ashau watersheds. Two large hill-masses

North Vietnamese women soldiers run ammunition and grenades down a trench during the defence of Base Area 611. Communist combat and logistics troops were intermingled in what they considered to be a safe haven from Free-World-Forces ground attacks. (PAVN)

**Marine Rifleman, Vietnam**
(See text commentary for detailed captions)

1STBATTALION 9TH MARINES

THE WALKING DEAD

A

Recruit and Drill Instructor,
Marine Corps Recruit Depot, USA

B

Advanced Training,
Infantry Training Regiment, USA

c

D

Personal Equipment, US Marine Corps M41 and M61 Patterns
(See text commentary for detailed captions)

SIGNAL ILLUMINATION,GROUND
PARACHUTE, M127, WHITE STAR
(HAND HELD)

M 18
SMOKE
VIOLET

PB-42-59

E

2f

2g

2e

4

2d 2c 2b

2h

2a

3

1

2i

Marine Machine Gunner, Vietnam
(See text commentary for detailed captions)

F

Personal Equipment, US Army M56 and M67 Patterns (See text commentary for detailed captions)

Fire Support Base, Operation Dewey Canyon

Fire-fight,
Operation Dewey Canyon

The Cost, Operation Dewey Canyon

J

The Victor, Operation Dewey Canyon

Navy Medical Corpsman, Vietnam (See text commentary for detailed captions)

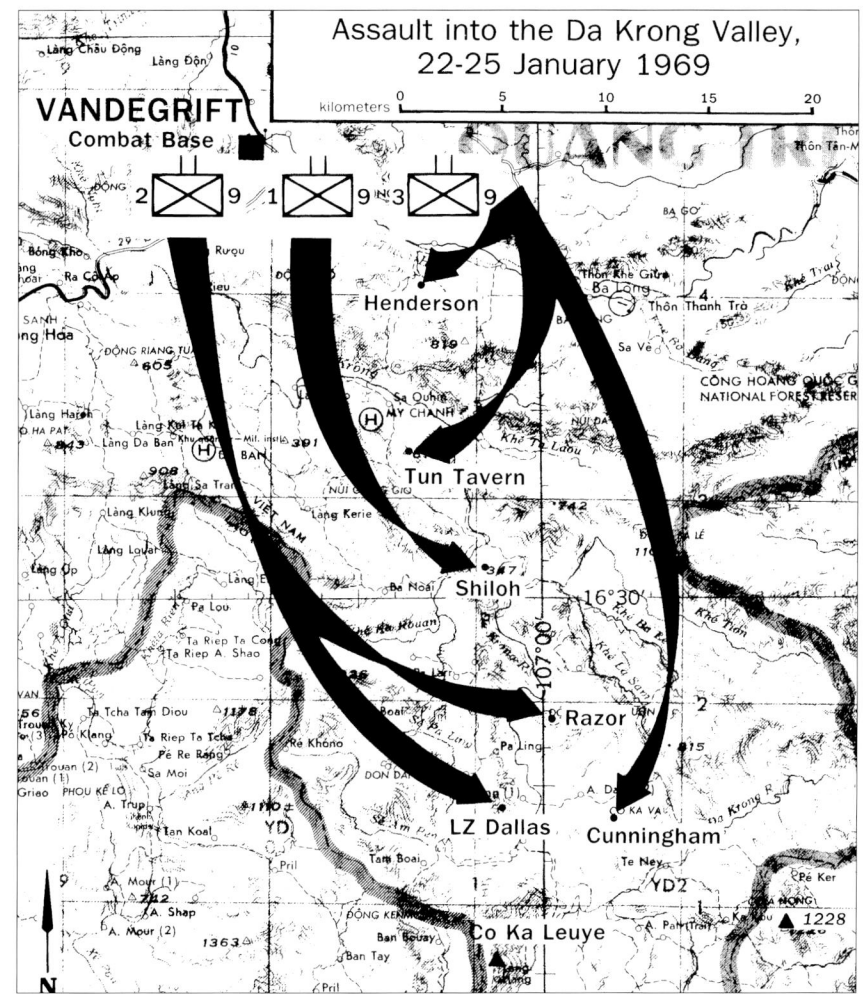

## Assault into the Da Krong Valley, 22-25 January 1969

Da Krong Valley, South Vietnam.
(MCHC)

dominated the apex of these valleys, Tam Boi and Co A Nong (Hills 1224 and 1228 respectively from their altitudes on the map), through which Routes 922 and 548 curved. For the infantry, this meant fighting uphill from 600 feet to final objectives of over 3,600 feet, covering an average horizontal distance of just four miles!

During the January to March monsoon season, temperatures were between 71 and 51 degrees – cool compared to the 100-degree temperatures of the lowlands. No significant rainfall occurred, but there were overcast skies and drizzle, with fog and clouds along the mountains and ravines. Barrow recalled that they "experienced unfavorable weather over fifty percent of the time" and that it "stalled or slowed the momentum of our attack and robbed us of our options".

Headquarters for 9th Marines was at Vandegrift Combat Base. Its battalions assembled there prior to 'D-Day' to rest, refit and rearm. A logistics support area was located at Vandegrift, with all classes of supplies moved by 3rd Shore Party Battalion. The regiment was supported by LtCol Joseph R. Scoppa's 2/12 artillery battalion, an engineer company and aircraft from the 1st Marine Aircraft Wing and the US Army 101st Airborne Division. Additional units from the 2nd ARVN and 3rd Marine Regiments were later brought into the operation.

Dewey Canyon kicked off on 18 January with the 9th and 12th Marines establishing fire support bases and blocking positions on three previously held hill-tops – Henderson, Tun Tavern and Shiloh. "Built by engineers, defended by the infantry and manned by artillery", the fire support base was an example of Marine flexibility, according to 3rd Engineer Battalion's operations officer, Maj Robert V. Nicoli. Basically, fire support bases were rapidly built artillery positions that allowed infantry to operate within a protective fan of fire that overlapped with other bases in order to fight in forests, jungles and mountains where ground movement was limited. Infantry moved forward in a classic 'fire and manoeuvre' of forces, rapidly abandoning bases that were no longer needed.

With artillery fire and air strikes for openers, Lt Wesley L. Fox's Alpha Company landed by helicopter at Shiloh on 21 January, starting the war for Cpl Smith's fire-team. Not knowing what to expect, the team left the helicopter at the double and took its place in the squad's section of the perimeter, with orders to "spread out, spread out!" The bombs and shells had torn the already constructed parapets and ammunition berms to pieces and everything had a damp mouldering feel.

Murphy and Valdez went down the side of the hill 'to make a head call', which ended with a cursing Murphy crashing down the slope into barbed wire with his trousers around his ankles. "Honest corporal, I got bamboo in my ass," he said to Smith, who was not impressed by Murphy's inability to defecate off the side of a hill.

Fire Support Base Shiloh proved to have been a 'vacation' for Alpha Company as Dewey Canyon unfolded and they were

The 2nd Battalion, 9th Marines moved into Laos to secure the right flank of the operation as the regiment entered Base Area 611. This squad moves down Route 922 to disrupt traffic into the battle area. (DOD)

left to guard two 105mm howitzer batteries and a 10-day supply of ammunition, rations and batteries moved forward from Vandegrift. Working parties improved and built fighting holes, bunkers and barbed wire obstacles. Mines, grenades and flares were installed. Observation posts were manned during the day and listening posts outside the lines at night, with two-man teams using field telephones and flares to warn of attack. The presence of ammunition and fuel meant there could be no open fires. Bunkers were dark and musty, beds were whatever was available to keep off the ground, and there were no windows or electricity. For company there were gnats, mosquitos, mice and rats. There was insufficient water for shaving or cooking, and not much more for drinking. Supplies were not plentiful and hot meals a distant memory; most living on canned rations. Mail was infrequent at best, tossed from the resupply helicopters in brightly coloured sacks.

Benotz had been sending his $73 overseas and combat pay to his girlfriend to make car payments. Shortly after arriving at Shiloh, a sack of mail brought him a letter from the finance company repossessing the automobile for non-payment and a 'Dear John' letter from his girl saying she was now married and would not be writing any more. Benotz tore these up and pinned the pieces to the company bulletin board to the cat-calls of "Get some!" from the headquarters clerks. Joe's comments were unprintable.

Enemy threats against these fixed positions were from 'stand off' and sapper attacks. The latter were special NVA units designed to conduct raids. The 3rd Marine Division chief-of-staff related that they used unobserved approaches – such as through the rubbish dump – with supporting mortar fire, backed at the last moment by RPGs, Chicom grenades, satchel charges and bangalore torpedoes to cover assaults made with utmost speed, keeping the defenders in their bunkers while the sappers hit ammunition stores, gun positions, fire direction and communication centres. Clearance patrols went out daily, and one platoon routinely left Shiloh for the small river at its foot in order to bathe, with due regard for security in 'Indian country'. Lieutenant Fox recalled that they would wind up their day by throwing grenades in the deep holes of the river and simply wading out and picking up the fish that floated to the top.

Valdez and Murphy attended church-call when a chaplain arrived, mainly

Closing in on the objective from the left flank were infantrymen from 3rd Battalion, 9th Marines moving up a battle-scarred slope in the Ashau Valley complex. Leathernecks advancing against the enemy-held mountain-top near the Laotian border dubbed the peak 'Tiger Mountain.' (DOD)

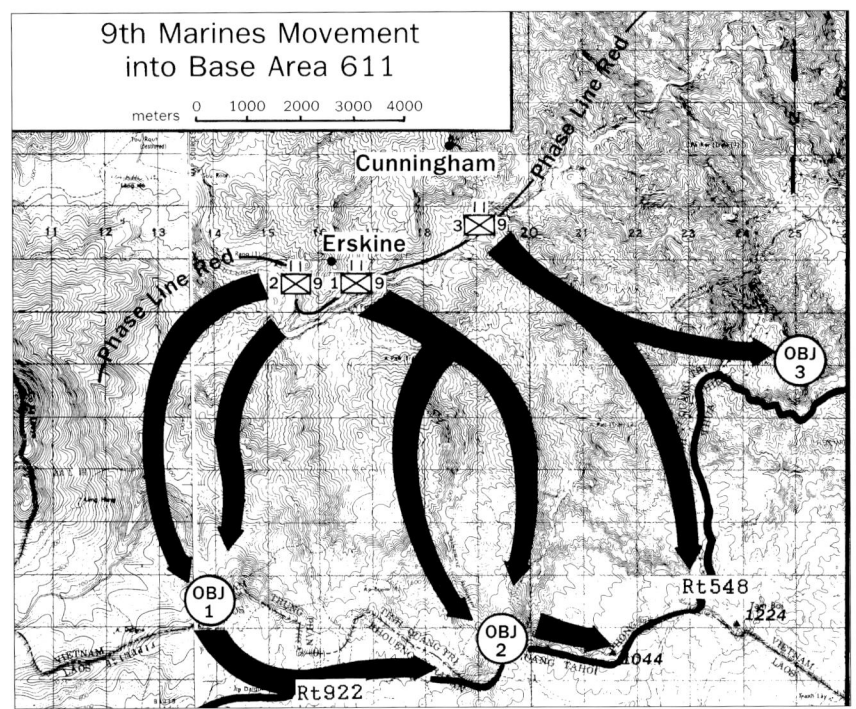

## 9th Marines Movement into Base Area 611

meters
0 1000 2000 3000 4000

Cunningham

Erskine

Phase Line Red

OBJ 3

OBJ 1

OBJ 2

Rt 548

1224

1044

Rt 922

VIETNAM
LAOS

**Base Area 611, South Vietnam and Laos. (MCHC)**

to get away from the company gunny and his never ending working parties. The rustic chapel was full, providing a tempting target, and the reading provoked a rejoinder picked up in–country: "Ye though I walk through the valley of the shadow of death I will fear no evil cuz I'm the meanest mutha in the valley."

On 22 January the regiment flew LtCol George C. Fox's 2/9 forward to secure Fire Support Base Razor and Landing Zone Dallas, to move closer to the enemy. Fire and air control agencies were established there and the 9th Marines were now fully committed. Two days later LtCol Elliot R. Laine's 3/9 assaulted the ridge for Fire Support Base Cunningham, a further 6,500 yards beyond Razor. This was home for the forward regimental command post, field hospital and logistics support group.

The fire support bases mounted 155mm howitzers, 105mm howitzers and 4.2 inch mortars. The artillery fan now extended six miles south and southwest to the limits of the operation area. From here, close air support took 30–45 minutes to call in and a helicopter some 45–60 minutes to arrive if the enemy and weather permitted. Because of the enemy anti-aircraft defences in Base Area 611, it was decided to attack cross-country rather than risk an airborne assault onto final objectives – One, Two and Three.

As initial gambits were being completed, 2/9 and 3/9 cleared the areas around the fire support bases and then advanced to Phase Line Red along the Da Krong River. An outlying company position, Fire Support Base Erskine, was built, and both battalions made light contact with screening forces from units they had believed to be further south. By 2 February an NVA field hospital had been overrun, a heavy company engagement had been fought by 2/9 in rain and fog on Hill 1175, Fire Support Base Cunningham had been shelled by 122mm guns and the bad weather had restricted air support. Company G was the most exposed and encountered a large enemy force as it pulled closer to friendly lines. Rain alternated with drizzle and fog, visibility was reduced to yards, and the ceiling to zero as hard red soil became mud.

Barrow decided to hold what ground the regiment had until things improved, and units sat in defensive positions in the rain, with resupply conducted by parachute drops from radar-guided helicopters and C130 transports. Nine days of poor weather cost them the impetus and gave the enemy time to prepare. On 10 February the weather cleared enough for LtCol George W. Smith's 1/9 to be helicoptered forward to Fire Support Base Erskine to take its place on Phase Line Red for the move from the Da Krong Valley up into Base Area 611. The 9th Marines was now on a line from west to east – 2/9, 1/9 and 3/9; each battalion with a zone of action three miles wide and assigned terrain objectives some four to five miles to the southwest.

On 12 February 1/9 ran into an NVA force soon after leaving Erskine. Artillery fire and manoeuvre by three companies killed 25 of the enemy. The other battalions met with machine-gun, mortar and recoilless rifle fire-fights as they advanced. On 17 February a sapper attack hit Cunningham, which was defended by 2/12 and M Company, leaving 37 bodies behind, 13 within the base itself; however, four Marines had died and another 46 were wounded.

Foot travel brought an all-encompassing cycle of demanding movement or rest, heat and damp, cold and damp, and exposure to the elements 24 hours a day. During the day, two companies advanced up the ridge lines alongside each other, with another company following. The lead units would attack and the rear units would move to the flanks or establish a landing zone for mortar support, resupply and medical evacuation. Companies rotated through these tasks as the situation permitted. At night, the companies stopped and established defensive perimeters.

Within Black's squad, Cpl Smith proved a competent team leader who saw that his replacements survived the transition into combat with a mixture of force and shrewdness – "attention to detail and mental alertness" was his litany to get their "heads and asses wired together". By example, he demonstrated how to adjust individual equipment, carry rifles and move in a staggered column or extended line. Economy of effort was used during halts, meals and in rigging expedient poncho shelters at night. Benotz, Valdez and Murphy were able to stay awake on watch without excitement or to fall asleep at the first opportunity. All that was needed was a 'baptism of fire' to prove their worth as riflemen.

Alpha Company experienced a number of heavy fire-fights, shortages of water and rations, and exhaustive patrols; it then recalled the 'good old days' back on Shiloh. Heavy fighting occurred between 18 and 22 February, mostly in 1/9's sector. Company A hit an entrenched platoon on a ridge three miles from Erskine, and the NVA "appeared to want to hold their position at all costs". The position was overrun and 30 Communists were killed. The next morning Company C moved through Alpha and killed as many on an adjacent hill. Lieutenant Archie Biggers' platoon was on "a really well-camouflaged road, about twelve feet wide and better made than anything I had ever seen" when it walked into two 122mm guns and 30 enemy fighting positions

Alpha Company Marines pinned down in dense growth to await the outcome of the fire fight ahead. Those not engaged took advantage of the delay in movement this offered to take a break and would continue the fight when called forward. (USNI)

(Terry). Charlie attacked and captured the two guns and prime movers, and Alpha then passed through to secure trucks and ammunition stockpiles. The 88 NVA killed were balanced against seven Marines dead and 44 wounded.

As battalions neared the border with Laos, Barrow sought permission to cut Route 922, which was being used to move enemy units in and out of the battle area, despite artillery, fighter bomber and B52 Stratofortress attacks. It fell to 2/9 to cross the border and ambush traffic on this critical route with infantry, which it did on 21 and 22 February – a story in itself.

By now there was concern about the general level of fatigue on the ground after four weeks of operations. The rugged terrain, tension of combat and lack of sleep was beginning to tell – in high pulse rates and dehydration. Company and platoon commanders knew that tired riflemen were careless and likely to forget good movement and security techniques as a result.

On 22 February, Alpha Company won its commander the Medal of Honor (one of five awarded the 9th Marines during the fighting). As the company neared the border in the centre of the regiment's advance, 1st Platoon pushed an enemy squad out of well-positioned bunkers. Since things looked quiet, Lt Fox radioed the battalion to send a detail down to the creek to get much needed water for headquarters and Charlie companies. The 20 men sent for water came under mortar and machine-gun fire, and 1st Platoon went to cover them, kicking off the last heavy engagement of Dewey Canyon.

After Sgt Black showed Cpl Smith where to go on the exposed flank across an open trail, Smith came back and shouted "Benotz with me! Valdez, Murphy, a magazine each, shoot like hell until we're across." He told Valdez and Murphy to follow as soon as they had changed magazines. Smith's final words were: "I will see you on the other

BELOW **Sgt Black directs Cpl Smith to take his team across an open area within a Communist defensive position at Dewey Canyon's climax. Fire and movement in the face of enemy fire was the classic test of infantry in combat. (DOD)**

BOTTOM **Serious casualties required medical evacuation, a medevac, where speed was essential for treatment of an emergency nature. A CH46 from HMM-262 touches down on an improvised landing zoned to receive a litter case carried by his fellow Marines. If halted by weather or enemy action, then the wounded did not get out. (DOD)**

side", as he and Benotz broke cover. As Valdez and Murphy raised up to shoot, machine-gun fire and Chi-com grenades blew a storm of fragments and debris into their faces and eyes from the direction the team leader had gone. They both flinched, and Valdez emptied a magazine without raising his head to aim. By the time Murphy lifted up to fire, Smith and Benotz were gone in the smoke and dust. A helmet lay rocking on the dirt trail surface and leaves and debris drifted down. Sgt Black came to see what was going on, bringing the other team for support as the fire-fight continued with grenade and mortar blasts.

After pushing through triple-canopy, undergrowth and banana groves, Lt Malone's men had hit a company-size defensive position, supported from high ground by rocket launchers and mortars. The 3rd and 2nd Platoons were soon committed in fighting that was so close that artillery and air support could not be used effectively.

The company executive officer took over 2nd Platoon when its commander went down, but was later hit himself. The command group was hit by mortars, killing or wounding everyone, but Lt Fox continued to move through the hazardous area, coordinating aircraft support with the activities of his men. In a final effort, small arms and grenades drove the enemy back. Wounded again in this assault, Fox reorganised his company into a defensive stance. Delta Company came up from behind the NVA position and the two companies linked up to evacuate the casualties – 11 killed and 72 wounded. One of those evacuated was Benotz with a chest wound; Benotz had not seen Smith after he had been hit and a body was not spotted. Some 105 NVA dead were counted, along with 25 crew-served weapons. Murphy found certificates and medals on one corpse that indicated he had killed an NVA war hero. More of these were located as the battlefield was swept clean.

On the regiment's left flank, 3/9 had advanced along Route 548, uncovering maintenance installations and fuel depots. The battalion cleared Hill 1228 (called Tiger Mountain by the Marines) and by 23 February had seized 122mm guns, prime movers, ammunition, a hospital and an underground headquarters complex. Fire Support Base Turnage was established on the Tiger Mountain hill complex to cover this phase of the fighting.

At the border, 1/9 re-oriented its march along Route 548 towards Hill 1044, where on 26 February Delta Company found one of the largest supply depots captured during the war – over 100 tons of munitions and 737 weapons. The next few days were spent recovering this materiel and destroying the complex – a massive effort which required two companies.

On the regiment's right

In the aftermath of battle, a navy medical corpsman examines surviving NVA prisoners, all of whome were injured and captured in the base area as the Communists withdrew into Laos. Most of the enemy were killed in action. (DOD)

flank, 2/9 swung through Laos until 1 March, covering 5,500 yards in five days – killing 48 enemy, capturing 20 tons of food, ammunition and two 122mm guns. This move blocked Route 922 at the time when 1/9 and 3/9 were pushing from the other side. This brought the operation to an end and a phased withdrawal began, and continued until 18 March, returning units by helicopter to the Vandegrift Combat Base. Communist forces up to company-size continued to attack in the Tiger Mountain area. The last unit to withdraw was 1st Battalion, 9th Marines and the survivors of Smith's fire-team; they left still under heavy mortar and anti-aircraft fire from Base Area 611's tenants.

The Dewey Canyon engagements killed 1,617 North Vietnamese soldiers (more were estimated killed by supporting fire) and took only five prisoners. The captured base area yielded 1,223 small arms, 104 machine-guns, 26 mortars, 73 anti-aircraft guns, 16 artillery pieces, 92 trucks and 14 bulldozers. Completing the haul were more than 800,000 rounds of ammunition – from small arms to artillery, 2,920 land mines, 800 pounds of explosives, 110 tons of rice and two tons of salt.

Marine casualties for the same period were 130 dead, 932 wounded and one missing. The operation had been supported by 461 close air support missions delivering 2,000 tons of ordnance and some 134,000 rounds of artillery fire. Helicopters had flown some 1,200 sorties to move 9,121 troops and 1,533,597 pounds of cargo, with the loss of one aircraft. For seven weeks enemy resupply and infiltration were blocked and pre-empted, as were major Communist attacks for the year, so tactical and operational success was achieved. The 9th Marines earned a unit citation for the most successful independent regimental operation of the conflict, retaining their reputation for hard fighting under rugged conditions as "a Marine regiment of extraordinary cohesion, skill in mountain warfare and plain heart". The regimental commander felt the battle was "regarded by many as the most unusual, challenging and successful large-scale operation of the Vietnam War". The credit for this success went to individual Marines, described by one of their battalion commanders as "hard corps – well trained and led, motivated to the highest degree, and undemanding of creature comforts".

Riflemen from Alpha Company stay alert as they move out onto Route 548 in the NVA base complex at the close of Operation Dewey Canyon. The ammunition cans hold extra rifle or machine gun ammunition carried for quick distribution. (DOD)

### Medal of Honors, 9th Marines, Operation Dewey Canyon

| | |
|---|---|
| LCpl Thomas P. Noonan | G Co, 5 February 1969* |
| LCpl Thomas E. Creek | I Co, 13 February 1969* |
| 1stLt Wesley L. Fox | A Co, 22 February 1969 |
| Cpl William D. Morgan | H Co, 25 February 1969* |
| PFC Alfred M. Wilson | M Co, 3 March 1969* |

\* Posthumous

# GROUPS AND ORGANISATIONS

### The Regiments Depart

Starting in July with the 9th Marines, the entire 3rd Marine Division had moved to Okinawa by November 1969. The 9th Marines continued to provide the Special Landing Force of the Seventh Fleet until the Vietnam War was finally over, in 1975. In 1979 its battalions returned to the United States on unit rotation, while the regimental headquarters remained overseas. These battalions served in the Persian Gulf and Somalia in 1990 and 1991. With the reduction in forces in the post Cold War defence structure, the 9th Marines' regimental headquarters was deactivated in July 1994, on the 50th anniversary of its landing on Guam in World War Two. The member battalions soon followed, and the 'Striking Ninth' was regulated to the history books until needed again. On 9 September 1995, at the 53 Area of Camp Pendleton, California, the older, wiser and heavier Joe Benotz and Juan Valdez watched the retirement of the colours for the 1st Battalion, carried by Marines who had not even been born when they had served in Operation Dewey Canyon. Of the others, Leroy Black remained in the Marine Corps until retirement, Pat Murphy died in a bar brawl soon after returning home, and Mike Smith was listed "killed-in-action, body-not-recovered".

### Marine Corps Historical Foundation

This organisation promotes, through the encouragement of the study of Marine Corps history and traditions, a deeper understanding of the historical role of the United States Marine Corps and the men and women who have served in it. It offers awards, grants and scholarships, and publishes a directory and newsletter. Membership is open to all interested in the history of the Corps. Contact P.O. Box 420, Quantico, Virginia 22134.

**Alpha Company Marines uncover the spoils of war from Operation Dewey Canyon in the form of 82mm mortar ammunition in one of many buried caches found throughout Base Area 611 near the Laotian border. (DOD)**

### 3rd Marine Division Association

This is a fraternal group founded in 1949 to hold annual reunions, raise funds for division causes and to publish a directory and newsletter. It is open to all Marines and corpsmen who served with the division. Contact P.O. Box 297, Dumfries, Virginia 22026.

### 1/9, 2/9, 3/9 Marines Networks

These are fraternal groups to meet the needs of Vietnam veterans of the 9th Marines through reunions and mailing lists.

Contact: 1st Bn 9th Marine Network, c/o 1152 Kensington Avenue, Plainfield, New Jersey 07060; 2nd Bn, 9th Marine Network, c/o P.O. Box 527, Waldo, Florida 32694; 3rd Bn, 9th Marines Network, c/o 33752 31st Avenue SW, Federal Way, Washington 98023.

Vietnam, like Korea, was fought in the shadow of World War Two, by veterans in senior ranks who thought it not much of a war, "but it was all we've got" and they soldiered on. The younger riflemen did not necessarily share this view: they saw it instead as their 'big show'. This led to a certain amount of dissatisfaction when the war ended, mitigated by personnel assignment policies that put them back into society as individuals without a suitable transition. The war's aftermath was felt strongest by these Marine veterans, who believed "America broke our heart" by denying them either victory or recognition.

Along with the obvious costs of the war, one unforeseen aspect was post-traumatic stress disorder and the impact this had on families and society. This might not be as unique as was first thought. One psychiatrist recently argued that the same sobering impact of war was depicted in Homer's *Iliad*, combat trauma and the undoing of character (Shay). Most veterans readjusted to society in the same way they handled combat, by their own efforts and with their friends and families, but the memory of those days and events remained long after their passing.

Napoleon correctly recognised that it is with bits of coloured ribbon that "one leads men". During the Vietnam War, medals and ribbons were awarded for valour, merit and service. While not a major concern in combat, the impact of the equitable distribution of decorations and awards was of concern in the war's aftermath. Perceptions existed that awards were based on rank, and that an officer had had to be present for

A Marine and corpsman examine a 122mm gun, the largest type captured in South Vietnam. The NVA soldiers had tried to swing the gun from facing down the Ashau Valley to an alternative firing position when overrun by the attacking 9th Marines. The Communists blew the barrel off and left the piece. (DOD)

It took two rifle companies to manhandle supplies to waiting helicopters, some of the tons of enemy ammunition seized during the operation. Marines carry 122mm ammunition through a platoon position littered with water bottles and ration boxes. (DOD)

a heroic deed to be recognised. The 9th Marines earned five Medal of Honors during Dewey Canyon, out of a total of 57 awarded to Marines during the entire war. Vietnam veterans of 1st Battalion recall with pride the more than 43 named operations that saw an estimated 600 battalion members killed and 4,000 wounded to earn the Purple Heart, America's oldest decoration. The Combat Action Ribbon was instituted during Vietnam for participation in battle and was also a personal award earned by Marines.

Unit awards went to specified organisations for significant accomplishment in combat; in Vietnam the 9th Marines earned two Presidential Unit Citations, two Navy Unit Commendations, two Meritorious Unit Commendations, and Vietnamese Gallantry Cross and Civil Actions unit citations.

Individual service awards included the National Defense Medal, the Vietnam Service Medal and the Vietnamese Campaign Medal – the three basic 'I was there' ribbons of the conflict. In addition, enlisted Marines earned the Good Conduct Medal for three years of continuous exemplary active service (or 'without getting caught', said cynics!).

# MUSEUMS AND COLLECTIONS

**Marine Corps Historical Centre**

Located at Building 58, Washington Navy Yard, in Washington D.C., this is the Marine Corps archival and museum facility. It is the starting point for anyone researching Vietnam and any other period of Corps history. It houses a museum which includes exhibits pertaining to the Vietnam era.

**Marine Corps Air-Ground Museum**

A branch of the historical centre located at Brown Field, Marine Corps Base, Quantico, Virginia. The Air-Ground Museum displays large artifacts that include armour, artillery and aircraft; as well as period uniforms and small arms. At present these are in three hangars with exhibits up to the Korean War. Vietnam era exhibits are planned. One of the 122mm guns captured by 1/9 is there, while another is at Fort Sill, Oklahoma. The museum also houses the Marine Corps Research Center, which includes a library and an excellent archive with Vietnam material.

## Vietnam Veterans Memorial

The Vietnam Veterans Memorial was dedicated on Veterans' Day Weekend in 1982. Located in Washington D.C. on The Mall near the Lincoln Monument, it is a series of black granite slabs arranged as a wall, with the 58,182 names of the dead and missing from the war. It includes two sculptures depicting three servicemen and women in period uniforms and equipment. The monument was intended to separate the US policy during the war from the issue of those who served as an act of national reconciliation. The cost of the monument was raised through contributions and it is administered by the National Park Service.

## Collecting

After a tour in Vietnam, an individual returned to the United States in a service uniform. Few Marines were in a position – or cared – to bring clothing and equipment home afterwards. On Okinawa there were piles of worn jungle utilities and boots left in heaps outside the huts used for processing personnel back home. Customs and military police discouraged efforts to bring anything else home or even to mail articles back.

Marines generally kept the utility cap, belt and jungle boots which were worn at their next duty station to proclaim status as returning warriors. Since these items were usually unsightly, this lasted until an officer or noncommissioned officer ran the Marine down and told them to send the stuff home. If an individual stayed in the Corps, these items were soon worn out or thrown away. At the time there was not much sentiment attached to clothing and equipment, with the exception of the above items and possibly the Ka-Bar knife. Photographs and captured enemy belongings were valued as souvenirs, and officers kept maps and notebooks as well.

With one third of the Marine Corps in Southeast Asia during this time, the bulk of personal clothing and equipment produced was used elsewhere. At best, a collector will be able to determine an individual item's date of manufacture or contract from markings on the piece. Illustrated are custody and war trophy documents that can authenticate items as Marine Corps issue and captured.

War Trophy DD Form 603-1 – this was used to give an individual permission to keep captured enemy items that had been screened for intelligence value, including some weapons. (MCHC)

WAR TROPHY REGISTRATION/AUTHORIZATION

INSTRUCTIONS: This form will be prepared for all types of war trophies. If trophy is a firearm, DD Form 603 will also be prepared.

Theater and inclusive period of service in overseas command
3D MARINE DIVISION IN THE FIELD - VIETNAM   (OCT67- OCT68)

| Name of Owner | Service Number | Grade/Rank |
|---|---|---|
| TUOTS, WILLIAM P. | 2103426 USMC | CORPORAL |

| Organization | Permanent Home Address |
|---|---|
| H&S COMPANY, 2ND BATTALION, 9TH MARINES, 3D MARINE DIVISION | 155 - 12 32ND AVENUE FLUSHING, N.Y. |

DESCRIPTION OF WAR TROPHY

Describe Item(s)
1 E-TOOL   1 PICK   1 MAGAZINE POUCH   1 STEEL HELMET
1 CHICOM POUCH   1 CANTEEN WITH COVER   1 AMMO POUCH

Serial Number or Identifying Mark
NONE

| Date | Typed Name, Grade and Organization of Authenticating Off. |
|---|---|
| 31 OCT 68 | B. K. JACKSON, CAPTAIN, USMC, G-2 COLLECTIONS OFFICER, |

| Station | Signature   3D MARINE DIVISION |
|---|---|
| DONG HA COMBAT BASE - RVN | |

DD Form 603-1, 1 Jul 65

56

# GLOSSARY

ACTUAL, SIX, SKIPPER – commanding officer
ARTY – artillery
ARVN – Army of the Republic of Vietnam
CHARLIE, NGYUEN – the enemy
CHOW – food
COMM – communications
CONUS, THE WORLD – Continental United States
CP – command post
CROTCH – the Marine Corps
DOC, BAC SE – medical corpsman
FMF – Fleet Marine Force
GRUNT – combat infantryman
HEAD – toilet
HIGH AND TIGHT – short haircut
HUMP – forced march
HQMC – Headquarters Marine Corps
ICTZ – I Corps Tactical Zone
KIA – killed in action
LIFER – career enlisted
LZ – landing zone
MACV – US Military Advisory Command Vietnam
MAF – Marine Amphibious Force
MIA – missing in action
NVA – North Vietnamese Army
SHORT TIMER – first-term enlisted or end of tour
VC, VIET CONG – Vietnamese Communist
VILLE – village or town
WASTE, POP, GET SOME – to kill
WIA – wounded in action

# BIBLIOGRAPHY

Appy, Christian G., *Working-Class War*, Chapel Hill (1993)
Barrow, MajGen Robert H., 'Operation Dewey Canyon', *Gazette*, pp84-89 (November 1981)
Commandant of the Marine Corps, *Dewey Canyon*, video (Washington D.C.)
Davis, 1stLt Gordon M., 'Dewey Canyon: All Weather Classic', *Gazette*, pp32-40 (September 1969)
Dawson, Capt David A., *The Impact of Project 100,000 on the Marine Corps* (Washington D.C. 1995)
Fleming, Dr V. Keith, 'Welcome to the Marines', *The Marines*, pp8-15 (Harrisburg 1989)
FMFM 6-5, *US Marine Rifle Squad*, various editions (Washington D.C.)
FMF Pacific, *A Marine's Guide to the Republic of Vietnam*, MCBul 3480 (1968)
Herr, Michael, *Dispatches* (New York 1977)
HQMC, *The 3rd Marine Division and its Regiments* (Washington D.C. 1983)
HQMC, *US Marine Corps Uniform Regulations*, various editions (Washington D.C.)
Lyles, Kevin, *Vietnam: US Uniforms in Colour Photographs* (London 1992)
Mares, William, *The Marine Machine* (New York 1971)
Nickerson, LtGen Herman, *Leadership Lessons and Remembrances from Vietnam* (Washington D.C. 1988)
Shay, Dr Johnathan, *Achilles in Vietnam* (New York 1994)
Simmons, BrigGen Edwin H., *Marines* (New York 1987)
Smith, Charles R., *US Marines in Vietnam*, 1969 (Washington D.C. 1988)
Terry, Wallace, *Bloods* (New York 1984)
TM10-276, *Hot Weather Clothing and Equipment* (Washington D.C. 1970)

RIGHT ABOVE **Riflemen admire their efforts with a captured M49 7.62mm machine gun and antiaircraft mount. Victory on the battlefield was defined by the seizure of territory, material, and eventual withdrawal. Other captured weapons are stacked for disposal with '1/9' marked water cans. (DOD)**

# THE PLATES

## A: MARINE RIFLEMAN, VIETNAM

Marines at this point in the war benefited from the previous four years of combat in terms of uniforms and equipment to fight with. Older Marine patterns were replaced by army-supplied equipment designed specifically for Southeast Asia. This fire-team leader, Cpl Smith, is going into the field wearing the height of fighting fashion – an M62 utility cover with his rank insignia pinned on the crown, and his M1 helmet is hanging off his 'ruck'. The camouflage utility uniform has lost its newness and is rolled at the sleeves and legs for ventilation while on the move in the tropics. Fabric and leather jungle boots were essential for the hot-wet conditions, complete with a dog-tag in the laces. His M55 armoured vest, a flak jacket, supports the weight of the pack and holds a rifle magazine that was removed from his M16 when not in the field (accidental discharges were frowned upon). He carries a salvaged demolitions bag to hold additional ammunition, grenades or mines; it could also carry rations if packs were not carried. The cartridge belt is an M56 pattern with ammunition pouches and canteens.

When rank was displayed on the utility uniform, it was in the form of metal pin-on insignia. Officers and enlisted rank at the company level were divided into commissioned officers, non-commissioned officers and enlisted men. Insignia were worn in matching pairs on the collars of jackets or shirts. They might also appear singly on the utility cover or on front or pocket of the utility jacket or armoured vest. Within a unit, the leaders were known well enough not to need to rely on any outward sign of authority.

The utility cap has a 1954 emblem applied by the manu-facturer, while the utility jacket was marked by individuals using a heat transfer decal or ink and stencil, with a larger emblem and the initials USMC to differentiate the Marines from other services which wore the same uniform.

As the jungle and camouflage utilities were theatre-issue clothing, markings were at the Marine's choosing. A last name and initials could be shown above the left breast pocket. Put there by rubber stamp, stencil, embroidery or hand-written. Helmet covers and flak jackets displayed graffiti depending upon what a unit would tolerate or what an individual could get away with. This was an unofficial means of identifying kit and of expressing opinion, and for identifying home towns or states, blood type or the length of time remaining in Vietnam. (After Kevin Lyles) **1** Armored vest. The army M52 type was also available and was constructed from kevlar fabric rather than the plates of the Marine M55. Since it fitted flush against the body, it was hotter to wear. **2** Sleeping shirt. This was kept dry in the pack until needed. Once stopped for the night, wet utilities could be removed and the dry polyester shirt worn until the damp clothing was put back on for the next day's move. It was also worn for warmth under the utility jacket in colder altitudes. **3** Jungle boots. The cure for the curse of heavy, wet leather combat boots was found in the popular 'hot weather tropical boot'. Even with them, care was required to control the problems of immersion foot. Side vents allowed water to drain out, and a plate in the sole offered some protection against penetration by spike booby-traps. **4** M1 helmet and cover. Another item of personal body armour favoured by the Americans because medical research from World War Two and the Korean War indicated it offered protection against injury from fragments.

Its utility in mobile situations was debated, but to Marine riflemen it was as essential as boots and a service rifle. The canvas cover was first used in World War Two and was a distinctive item of Marine equipment until the general adoption of helmet covers by the Department of Defense in 1962. **5** Lightweight tropical rucksack and contents. This rucksack replaced the Marine's M41 haversack and knapsack which were not suited to Vietnam service. Fighting gear was carried on the belt, but the pack was the rifleman's home in the field, and the contents of each varied, but revolved around the basics shown here: **a** underclothing, **b** towel, **c** poncho, **d** rations, **e** machete, and **f** air mattress. It did not take long to learn that weight and necessities needed to be balanced and mandated loads would often prevent either of these, since unit supplies were also carried. Plates E and G show additional individual equipment and munitions used. **6** Unofficial 'beer-can' crest for 1st Battalion, 9th Marines. This design originated during the Vietnam War and was used on patches, hats, shirts and coffee mugs. **7** M161A1 rifle; **8** MX-991/U flashlight used since the late war.

## B: RECRUIT AND DRILL INSTRUCTOR, MARINE CORPS RECRUIT DEPOT, USA

Like other historical elites, the Marines prided themselves on the severe training that took individuals from diverse backgrounds and circumstances and gave them a sense of common identity. By the mid-1960s, this took on a sharper edge with the return of combat veterans and the reduction in training time to maintain the level of manpower required to support the war. One element that continued to be used to obtain compliance was close order drill. A rather confused Pvt Murphy is being given individual instruction from his DI in the difference between left and right. While physical abuse by instructors was officially prohibited, DIs 'laid hands' on recruits to adjust uniforms or to assist in the learning process.

Uniforms were the most visible indicator of status between the two. Murphy wears a silver-painted helmet liner 'chrome dome', undershirt, M62 utility trousers and an M61 cartridge belt. The recruit is advertised by the ill-fitting newness of the uniform, lack of rank insignia and his trousers hanging over

his combat boots. Wearing of a full uniform was graduated to levels of performance. The drill instructor has a campaign hat with its four-dent Montana Peak, an outmoded issue that was limited to instructors and shooting team members. A 'duty' belt also indicates his billet. In contrast to the recruit, the sergeant's M62 utility uniform is starched and ironed to a stiff freshness, which necessitates several changes a day to maintain in humid weather. His boots and brass fittings were polished by recruits each night. (After William Mares)

## C: ADVANCED TRAINING, INFANTRY TRAINING REGIMENT, USA

Military occupational speciality skills were taught at both Camp Pendleton, California, and Camp Lejeune, North Carolina. In addition, most Vietnam-bound Marines passed through pre-deployment orientation at Camp Pendleton before going overseas, although this was not always the case as the war proceeded.

Orientation consisted of lecture, demonstration and application as the Marines were introduced to M16 rifles, 'jungle-lanes' and 'Vietnam villages'. These two Marines are practising the skill needed to search and clear a village with the help of costumed aggressors, including Pvt Valdez emerging from the 'spider-hole' with a PPSH submachine-gun in his hand. The Marines wear the M62 utility uniform that was standard in the States, with an abbreviated belt order limited to M61 magazine pouches for the M14 rifles carried. Valdez and his companion wear black 'pajama' clothing similar to that of rural peasants. Needless to say, the terrain and climate of southern California was very different from that of Southeast Asia, and the training facilities were the same ones that had been used for World War Two and Korea.

## D: ARRIVAL AND ASSIGNMENT, VIETNAM

For the majority of riflemen, this was the first time in the replacement pipeline that they were treated as something other than an anonymous group moved in mass from one destination to another. Once in-country, the assignment system narrowed their options until they arrived at a unit. In this case, Sgt Black rounds up replacements assigned to

**Success defined by the infantryman was moving to the rear with the gear and having all major body parts in place. This machine gunner catches up on his reading before going out the next time. The kit and uniform were worn for comfort if not style. (DOD)**

Alpha Company, 9th Marines – including Benotz, Valdez and Murphy. The whole system was set up for this, to put trained riflemen into the field against the enemy for the next 13 months, unless injury or death brought new replacements. Black wears the early jungle utilities; the replacements wear the later camouflage version, with M56 personal equipment and M16 rifles. Again, the contrast of experience and naivety is apparent. Those leaving at the end of their tour could be heard calling out: "You'll be sorry!"

## E: PERSONAL EQUIPMENT, US MARINE CORPS M41 AND M61 PATTERNS

**1** Intrenching tool; **2** M61 cartridge belt; **3** M61 cartridge pouches; **4** M44/45 canteen and cover; **5** M41 belt suspender straps; **6** Jungle first aid kit; **7** M44/45 canteen and cup; **8** M6 bayonet knife and scabbard; **9** M1 holster, automatic pistol; **10** M1911A1 pistol, .45 calibre; **11** Pistol magazine and pouch; **12** Grenade carrier for M26 hand-grenade; **13** M14 rifle magazine; **14** Fighting and utility knives made by Ka-Bar and case; **15** M67 hand-grenade; **16** M26 hand-grenade; **17** M18 smoke-grenade; **18** M94 incendiary-grenade; **19** M127 parachute flare.

## F: MARINE MACHINE GUNNER, VIETNAM

While riflemen were most common, other infantrymen played a significant tactical role. In the ground combat in Vietnam, the M60 machine-gun team provided the base of fire needed to manoeuvre rifle squads and formed the backbone of any defence. They operated in a flexible role using a bipod and in the fixed mode, firing from a tripod.

This machine-gunner is 'loaded for bear' for mobile operations. He carries lubricant and a toothbrush on his M1

For the 9th Marines, Operation 'Dewey Canyon' marked the end of the Vietnam War. With its departure on 14 July 1969, the 1st battalion loaded the USS *Paul Revere* for the three-day trip to Okinawa as part of President Nixon's redeployment programme. (DOD)

helmet. He totes the M60 'black bitch' with a 50-round 'teaser' belt loaded into the feed tray and has 200 rounds of ready ammunition slung across the M55 flak jacket, which is worn over an olive-green under shirt. The towel around his neck serves as a sweat rag and cushion. Other individual equipment consist of an M41 pack and poncho, a web belt to hold canteens and a holster for his M1911A1 pistol with a Ka-Bar fighting knife wedged behind. On his left hip is an M17 gas mask and case to protect him from chemicals that were used by both sides. His trousers are rolled above the boots for air circulation. The jungle boots are laced loose, with an identification tag for easy access.

The M60 was operated by a two-man team: the gunner and assistant gunner (or 'A' gunner). Others were assigned as 'ammo humpers', to carry additional belted 7.62mm ammunition. This required the gunner to carry a 24-pound weapon in addition to his personal equipment; his assistant carried another 33 pounds of accessories including a spare barrel; and ammunition weighed 6.5 pounds for each 100 rounds. **1** An 'assault pack' of 100 rounds of 7.62mm belted ammunition (one round tracer to four of ball) issued in a cardboard box and cloth bandolier and carried two per metal ammunition container or 'ammo can'. **2a** M60 machine-gun spare barrel-case and accessories; **2b** Bore brush; **2c** Chamber brush; **2d** Receiver brush;

**e** Combination wrench; **f** Ruptured cartridge extractor; **g** Handle; **h** Cleaning rod; rel-case;
**k** Asbestos glove; **3** The beer-can version of the 9th Marines regimental crest, designed in World War Two by regimental commander Col Lemuel C. Shepherd Jr. The design was used as the basis for informal equipment and clothing.

## G: PERSONAL EQUIPMENT, US ARMY M56 AND M67 PATTERNS

**1** M62 canteen; **2** M56 individual equipment belt; **3** M56 universal small arms ammunition case (M14); **4** M56 entrenching tool carrier; **5** M7 bayonet knife and scabbard; **6** M56 suspenders; **7** M56 combat field pack; **8** M62 canteen and M56 cover; **9** M56 case and compass; **10** M56 sleeping bag carrier; **11** M67 entrenching tool and carrier; **12** M56 universal small arms ammunition case (M16); **13** M16 rifle magazine; **14** M56 adapter assembly; **15** M67 universal small arms ammunition case (M16); **16** M16 automatic rifle bipod and accessory case; **17** M56 case and individual first aid field dressing; **18** 5.56mm ammunition and stripper clips; **19** 5.56mm ammunition bandolier; **20** M67 individual equipment belt with quick release buckle; **21** Rifle grenade sight case (M14); **22** M42 machete and M67 sheath; **23** M67 small arms cleaning kit; **24** M18 Claymore anti-personnel mine .

## H: FIRE SUPPORT BASE, OPERATION DEWEY CANYON

The airmobile operations by the 9th Marines established fixed fortified positions to provide helicopter and artillery support to infantry units moving by foot without supply lines in rugged mountain terrain. The fire support bases also provided command and control, communications and medical backing. They were subject to enemy attacks by fire and raids the longer they remained in one place. While not as primitive as in the manoeuvre companies, these outposts were still subject to harsh conditions and exposure to weather.

## I: FIRE-FIGHT, OPERATION DEWEY CANYON

The classic engagement for infantry in Vietnam was the close-range, violent and unpredictable fire-fight that saw opponents pitted against each other with small arms until one side or the other could bring to bear a decisive weight of supporting arms or manoeuvre. Weather, terrain and surprise were all critical influences for both sides, and the infantry's job was to fight, win or lose. In these conditions skill-at-arms, tenacity and effective small unit leadership were needed – to hit the deck, return fire and dominate the situation. A grenadier fires an M79 in support of his squad in the initial stages of a contact, while the riflemen seek to return effective fire under the control of the team leader on the right.

## J: THE COST, OPERATION DEWEY CANYON

Pte Benotz is treated for a sucking chest wound by 'Doc', a company corpsman who had a number of others to take care of while the company organised evacuation. Casualties were dead and wounded from enemy fire, friendly fire, and accidents in the maelstrom of combat. The appalling damage caused by projectiles, fragments, blast and concussion were magnified by the effects of weather, filth and evacuation. Navy corpsmen had to triage the injured and conduct the field surgery necessary to stabilise the wounded until they

could be evacuated to the rear for treatment – by helicopter if possible and by stretcher parties if necessary. The normal course of evacuation was along the same lines as ammunition, water and food being brought forward.

### K: THE VICTOR, OPERATION DEWEY CANYON

A Marine rifleman at the end of the day, in possession of the field in enemy territory, in this case on a blasted artillery prime mover in Base Area 611. Pte Murphy and his fire-team have accomplished the task of the infantry, to close with and destroy the enemy. Murphy gave a noncommittal look at a very dead Communist driver and pronounced: "Whose hill now, Charlie?" The score for his four-man unit was one missing, one wounded and two left to hold the ground until the 9th Marines withdrew from the area. These events in the first half of the year would be the highlight of their military 'careers'.

### L: NAVY MEDICAL CORPSMAN, VIETNAM

In each rifle platoon and company were individual field medics or hospital 'corpsmen' who were members of the US Navy. At this level the 'Doc' assumed fabled proportions with that of the squad leader and platoon commander. A recent veterans reunion was dedicated solely to 'grunt corpsmen' because of the impact they had at the small unit level. Navy medical doctors and staff ran aid stations at the battalion and regimental levels.

This platoon corpsman is dressed for the field the same as a Marine rifleman, and in fact often carried an M16 instead of the issue pistol. While his helmet, flak jacket, utility uniform and boots are prosaic, this corpsman is distinguished by a 'Unit One' bag and ammunition bandolier stuffed with extra field dressings. **1** Identification tags. One symbol of service was the issue of 'dog-tags', which stayed with a Marine throughout his service in case he was killed or wounded. The stamped aluminium plates were issued in pairs and worn on a metal chain around the neck. In the field a tag might be laced onto a boot. **2** Medical instrument and supply set, the Unit One, carried by platoon-level corpsmen with supplies to treat wounds and illness. The standard issue was modified to fit the unit's mission and circumstances – such as extra field dressings, morphine and plasma. It was worn, ready for use, across the chest with a general-purpose carrying strap. **3** Medical instrument kit, used in field surgery for life-saving procedures in addition to the Unit One. **4** Jungle first aid kit. It had plastic strip band aids, elastic gauze bandages, individual field dressings, water purification tablets, salt tablets, anti-chap stick, sodium chloride-sodium bicarbonate for burns, and an eye wash solution. Often these supplies would be unavailable and the case would be used to carry cigarettes and snacks instead. **5** First aid individual field dressing, carried to be used for one's own wounds. First aid was intended to clear airways, stop bleeding, treat for shock and protect the wound until medical treatment and evacuation could be arranged, often after the fighting was over. **6** A beer-can emblem for the 3rd Marine Division that was designed and worn in World War Two as a shoulder insignia. The three points of the tetrahedron symbolised the division's three infantry regiments and number.

# Notes sur les planches en couleur

**A** A ce stade de la guerre, les marines bénéficiaient des quatre années précédentes de combat au niveau des uniformes et du matériel de combat. Les modèles plus anciens avaient été remplacés par du matériel d'armée conçu spécifiquement pour l'Asie du sud-est. **1** Gilet pare-balles. **2** Chemise de nuit. **3** Bottes. **4** Casque et housse M1. **5** Sac à dos tropical léger et son contenu. **6.** Cimier officiers en forme de canette de bière pour le 1er bataillon, 9e Marines.

**B** Tout comme les autres élites historiques, les Marines étaient fiers de l'entraînement difficile qui prenait des individus venus de milieux et de situations très diverses et leur donnait un sens d'identité commune. L'un des éléments utilisés pour discipliner les recrues était la manoeuvre stricte en petits groupes. Le soldat Murphy désorienté reçoit une leçon particulière de son DI, qui lui explique la différence entre sa gauche et sa droite. Bien que les châtiments corporels aient été interdits officiellement, les instructeurs "levaient la main" sur les recrues pour ajuster leur uniforme ou pour accélérer le processus d'apprentissage.

**C** Au Camp Pendleton, en Californie et au Camp Lejeune, en Caroline du Nord, on enseignait des tactiques spéciales. Ces deux Marines s'entraînent à fouiller et évacuer un village avec l'aide d'agresseurs costumés dont le soldat Valdez, qui émerge du "spider hole", armé d'une mitrailleuse PPSH.

**D** Pour la majorité des fusiliers, c'était la première fois dans le pipeline des remplacements qu'on les traitait autrement qu'un groupe anonyme que l'on déplaçait en masse d'une destination à l'autre. Une fois sur place, le système des placements diminuait leurs options jusqu'à ce qu'ils arrivent à une unité. Dans ce cas, le sergent Black rassemble les remplaçants affectés à la Compagnie Alpha, 9e Marines, dont Benotz, Valdez et Murphy.

**E1** Pelle à tranchées; **2** cartouchière M61; **3** giberne à cartouches M61; **4** gamelle et couvercle M44/45; **5** bretelles de ceinture M41; **6** Trousse de secours dans la jungle; **7** gamelle et tasse M44/45; **8** couteau à baïonnette et poignard M6; **9** étui, pistolet automatique M1; **10** pistolet, calibre .45 M1911A1; **11** Chargeur et giberne pour pistolet; **12** Porte-grenade avec grenade à main M26; **13** chargeur de fusil M14; **15** Couteaux de combat et de cuisine fabriqués par Ka-Bar et étuis; **16** grenade à main M67; **17** grenade à main M26; **18** grenade fumigène M18; **19** grenade incendiaire M94; **20** Fusée éclairante pour parachute M127.

**F** Ce mitrailleur est "loaded for bear" (chargé pour le transport) pour les opérations mobiles. Il porte la "black bitch" (chienne noire) M60 avec une bande ou "teaser" de 50 cartouches chargée sur le plateau d'alimentation. Il porte aussi une bande de 200 cartouches sur son gilet pare-balles M55, qu'il porte par-dessus une sous-chemise vert olive. **1** Un "assault pack" de 100 cartouches de 7,62mm en bande (une balle traçante pour quatre balles) distribué dans une boîte en caton avec une bandoulière en tissu, porté deux à la fois dans un conteneur de munitions en métal ou "ammo can". **2a** Baril et accessoires de rechange pour une mitrailleuse M60; **2b** brosse à canon; **2c** brosse à chambre; **2d** brosse à récepteur; **2e** clé anglaise; **2f** extracteur de cartouches cassé; **2g** poignée; **2h** tige de nettoyage; **2i** carter de baril de rechange; **2j** baril de rechange; **2k** gant en amiante; **3** la version "canette de bière" du cimier régimentaire des 9e Marines.

**G1** Gamelle M62; **2** ceinture pour matériel individuel M56; **3** boîtier à munitions universel pour armes portatives M56 (M14); **4** porte-pelle à tranchées M56; **5** couteau à baïonnette et étui M7; **6** Bretelles M56; **7** paquetage de combat M56; **8** gamelle M56 et couvercle M56; **9** boîtier et boussole M56; **10** porte-sac de couchage M56; **11** pelle à tranchées et porte-pelle M56; **12** boîtier universel pour munitions d'armes portatives M56 (M16); **13** chargeur de fusil M16; **14** assemblage d'adaptateur M56; **15** boîtier universel pour munitions d'armes portatives M67 (M16); **16** pied pour fusil automatique M16 et boîte d'accessoires; **17** boîtier et pansement individuel de premier secours M56; **18** cartouches de 5,56mm et pattes de chargement; **19** cartouchière de balles de 5,56mm; **20** ceinture de matériel individuel M67 avec boucle à dégagement rapide; **21** viseur de grenade à fusil (M14); **22** machette M42 et étui M67; **23** kit de nettoyage d'armes portatives; **24** mine anti-personnel Claymore M18.

**H** Les opérations aéroportées des 9e Marines permirent d'établir des positions fixes fortifiées afin de fournir un soutien par hélicoptère et artillerie aux unités d'infanterie qui se déplaçaient à pied, sans ligne de ravitaillement, en terrain montagneux et difficile. Les bases de soutien d'artillerie fournissaient également commandement et contrôle, communications et soutien médical.

**I** Le combat classique de l'infanterie au Vietnam était le tir violent, imprévisible à courte portée, avec les ennemis qui se mesuraient aux armes portatives, jusqu'à ce que l'un ou l'autre des camps puisse remporter la victoire grâce au nombre d'armes à feu ou à des manoeuvres. Les conditions météo, le terrain et l'élément de surprise étaient tous des influences critiques pour les deux camps, et le travail de l'infanterie était de se battre, de gagner ou de perdre.

**J** Le soldat Benotz est traité pour une blessure grave à la poitrine par "Doc", un docteur de la compagnie qui avait d'autres blessés à soigner pendant que la compagnie organisait l'évacuation. Il y avait des morts et des blessés par feu ennemi, feu de leurs propres rangs et accidents durant l'ouragan du combat.

**K** Un fusilier des Marines à la fin de la journée, en possession du terrain en territoire ennemi, dans ce cas perché sur un gros véhicule d'artillerie détruit dans la Zone de Base 611. Le soldat Murphy et son équipe de fusiliers ont accompli le travail de l'infanterie, qui est de se refermer sur l'ennemi et de le détruire. Murphy lança un regard évasif au chauffeur communiste totalement mort et lança : "La colline de qui maintenant, Charlie ?".

**L** Ce membre de section est habillé pour le terrain de la même manière qu'un fusilier des Marines, et en fait portait souvent un M16 au lieu du pistolet réglementaire. **1** Étiquettes d'identification. Un symbole de service était la distributions de "dog-tags", qu'un Marine conservait toute sa carrière, si jamais il était blessé ou tué. **2** Trousse d'instruments et de produits médicaux portée prête à l'utilisation sur la poitrine, avec une lanière de transport polyvalente. **3** Kit d'instruments médicaux utilisé sur le terrain pour des opérations chirurgicales d'urgence, en plus de celle de l'unité. **4** Kit de premier secours dans la jungle. **5** Pansement individuel de premier secours, que chacun devait porter pour traiter ses propres blessures. **6** Emblème "canette de bière" de la 3e Division des Marines.

**64**

# Farbtafeln

**A** In dieser Phase des Krieges konnten die Marinetruppen in Bezug auf die Uniformen und die Kampfausrüstung die in den vorherigen vier Kriegsjahren gesammelten Erfahrungen nutzen. Die bisherigen Marine-Modelle wurden durch von der Armee gelieferte Ausrüstungen ersetzt, die eigens für Südostasien gedacht waren. **1:** Panzerweste. **2:** Schlafhemd. **3:** Dschungelstiefel. **4:** Helm M1 mit Helmbezug. **5:** Leichter Tropenrucksack mit Inhalt. **6:** Inoffizielles "Bierdosen"-Emblem des 1. Bataillons, 9th Marines.

**B** Wie andere herkömmliche Elitetruppen auch, waren die Marinetruppen stolz auf die strenge Ausbildung, die den Einzelnen von unterschiedlicher Herkunft und aus den verschiedensten Verhältnissen eine gemeinsame Identität gab. Ein Mittel, für Gehorsam zu sorgen, war der scharfe Drill. Der zuständige DI erteilt einem eher verwirrten Pvt Murphy Einzelunterricht, was den Unterschied zwischen links und rechts betrifft. Zwar war die körperliche Züchtigung offiziell untersagt, doch legten die DIs bei den Rekruten "Hand an", wenn es darum ging, die Uniform auszurichten oder den Lernprozeß etwas nachzuhelfen.

**C** Berufliche Fachkenntnisse für das Militär wurden sowohl im Camp Pendleton in Kalifornien als auch im Camp Lejeune in North Carolina vermittelt. Diese beiden Marineinfanteristen üben mit Hilfe verkleideter Angreifer die Fähigkeiten, die zur Durchsuchung und Räumung eines Dorfes erforderlich sind. Man sieht Pvt Valdez mit einer PPSH-Maschinenpistole in der Hand aus einem "Spinnenloch" kommen.

**D** Für den Großteil der Schützen war dies das erste Mal im Nachschub, daß sie nicht nur als anonyme Gruppe behandelt wurden, die en masse von einem Ort zum anderen geschickt wurde. Waren sie erst einmal vor Ort, so waren ihre Möglichkeiten durch das Zuteilungssystem beschränkt, bis sie bei einer Einheit angelangt waren. In diesem Fall trommelt Sgt Black Nachschubsoldaten zusammen, die der Alpha Company, 9th Marines, zugeteilt wurden - darunter auch Benotz, Valdez und Murphy.

**E 1** Schanzwerkzeug; **2** Patronengürtel M61; **3** Patronentaschen M61; **4** Feldflasche und Bezug M44/45; **5** Gürteltrageschlaufen M41; **6** Erste-Hilfe-Kasten für den Dschungel; **7** Feldflasche und Tasse M44/45; **8** Bajonettmesser und Scheide M6; **9** affter M1, Automatikpistole; **10** .45 Kaliber-Pistole M1911A1; **11** Pistolenmagazin und Tasche; **12** Granatenbehälter mit Handgranate M26; **13** Gewehrmagazin M14; **14** Kampf- und Mehrzweckmesser von Ka-Bar und Hülle; **16** Handgranate M67; **17** Handgranate M26; **18** Rauchgranate M18; **19** Brandgranate M94; **20** Fallschirm-Leuchtpistole M127.

**F** Dieser Maschinengewehrschütze ist für den mobilen Einsatz mit "tragbarer Last" ausgestattet. Er hat die "black bitch" M60 mit einem 50-Schuß "teaser"-Streifen, der an der Ladeöffnung schußfertig eingezogen ist, bei sich. Außerdem trägt er 200 Schuß Munition über der kugelsicheren Weste M55, unter der er ein olivgrünes Unterhemd trägt. **1** Eine "Angriffspackung" mit 100 Schuß gebündelter 7,62mm-Munition (pro vier Kugeln jeweils ein Leuchtspurgeschoß), in einer Schachtel verpackt mit einem Stoffbandolier, von der jeweils zwei in einem Munitionsbehälter aus Metall, der sogenannten "Munitionsdose", getragen wurden. **2a** Hülle für den Ersatzlauf des Maschinengewehrs M60 und Zubehör; **2b** Gewehrlaufbürste; **2c** Kammerbürste; **2d** Beckenbürste; **2e** Kombizange; **2f** Zange zum Lösen geplatzter Patronen; **2g** Griff; **2h:** Reinigungsstab; **2i** Hülle für den Ersatzlauf; **2j** Ersatzlauf; **2k** Asbest-Handschuh; **3** die "Bierdosen"-Version des Regimentsemblems der 9th Marines.

**G1** Feldflasche M62; **2** Gürtel für Einzelausrüstung M56; **3** Universal-Munitionsbehälter M56 für Handfeuerwaffen (M14); **4** Behälter für Schanzwerkzeug M56; **5** Bajonettmesser und Scheide M7; **6** Hosenträger M56; **7** Feldkampfgepäck M56; **8** Feldflasche M62 und Hülle M56; **9** Behälter und Kompaß M56; **10** Schlafsackbehälter M56; **11** Schanzwerkzeug und Behälter M67; **12** Universal-Munitionsbehälter M56 für Handfeuerwaffen (M16); **13** Gewehrmagazin M16; **14** Adaptersatz M56; **15** Universal-Munitionsbehälter M67 für Handfeuerwaffen (M16); **16** Zweibein für Automatikgewehr M16 und Zubehörbehälter; **17** Behälter M56 und individuelle Erste-Hilfe-Feldverband; **18** 5,56mm-Munition und Ladestreifen; **19** 5,56mm-Munitionsgürtel; **20** Koppel für Einzelausrüstung M67 mit Schnellöseschnalle; **21** Visierbehälter für Gewehrgranate (M14); **22** Machete M42 und Scheide M67; **23** Ausrüstung zur Reinigung von Handfeuerwaffen M67; **24** Claymore-Personenabwehrmine M18.

**H** Die "Airmobil"-Operationen der 9th Marines schufen feste, befestigte Positionen, die den Infanterieeinheiten, die in zerklüftetem Gebirgsterrain ohne Versorgungslinien zu Fuß unterwegs waren, Unterstützung mit Hubschraubern und Artillerie lieferten. Außerdem sorgten die Feuerstützpunkte für Befehle und Kontrolle, Kommunikation und ärztliche Versorgung.

**I** Der typische Einsatz der Infanterie in Vietnam war das heftige, unberechenbare Geschützfeuer aus nächster Nähe, bei dem die gegnerischen Seiten sich mit Handfeuerwaffen bekämpften, bis eine Seite zum entscheidenden Schlag mit weiterem Gewehrfeuer oder einem Manöver ausholen konnte. Auf beiden Seiten spielten das jeweilige Gelände, das Wetter und der Überraschungsfaktor eine wichtige Rolle, und die Aufgabe der Infanterie war es zu kämpfen, bis zum Sieg oder zur Niederlage.

**J** Pte Benotzs klaffende Brustwunde wird vom "Doc" versorgt, einem Mitglied der Kompanietruppe, der sich auch noch um eine Reihe anderer Verletzter zu kümmern hatte, während die Kompanie sich auf die Evakuierung vorbereitete. Die Gefallenen und Verletzten fielen in der Hitze des Gefechts dem feindlichen Geschützfeuer, dem eigenen Geschützfeuer und Unfällen zum Opfer.

**K** Ein Schütze der Marinetruppen am Ende des Tages im Besitz des Feldes auf feindlichem Gelände, in diesem Fall auf einem gesprengten Artilleriegefährt in der Base Area 611. Pte Murphy und seine Schützenmannschaft haben die Aufgabe der Infanterie erfüllt, nämlich den Feind zu stellen und zu vernichten. Murphy warf einen nichtssagenden Blick auf einen toten kommunistischen Fahrer und sagte: "Wem gehört der Hügel nun, Charlie?"

**L** Dieser Soldat eines Zugs ist genauso für das Feld gekleidet wie ein Schütze der Marinetruppen und hatte in der Tat anstelle der vorschriftsmäßigen Pistole oft ein M16 bei sich. **1** Erkennungsmarken. Ein Merkmal der Waffengattung war die Herausgabe von sogenannten "Hundemarken", Erkennungsmarken, die die Marinetruppen während ihrer gesamten Dienstzeit trugen, falls sie getötet oder verletzt würden. **2** Der ärztliche Instrumenten- und Versorgungssatz wurde einsatzbereit an einem Mehrzweckgurt quer über der Brust getragen. **3** Ärztliches Instrumentenkästchen, das im Feld zusätzlich zur "Unit One" bei lebensrettenden Eingriffen eingesetzt wurde. **4** Erste-Hilfe-Kasten für den Dschungel. **5** Individueller Erste-Hilfe-Feldverband, der zur Versorgung der eigenen Wunden mitgeführt wurde. **6** "Bierdosen"-Emblem der 3rd Marine Division.